OUTINGS

&

THE ACT

by Thomas Hescott and Matthew Baldwin

samuelfrench.co.uk

FOR AMATEUR PRODUCTION ENQUIRIES

UNITED KINGDOM AND WORLD
EXCLUDING NORTH AMERICA
plays@samuelfrench.co.uk
020 7255 4302/01

Each title is subject to availability from Samuel French,
depending upon country of performance.

THINKING ABOUT PERFORMING A SHOW?

There are thousands of plays and musicals available to perform from Samuel French right now, and applying for a licence is easier and more affordable than you might think

---

From classic plays to brand new musicals, from monologues to epic dramas, there are shows for everyone.

Plays and musicals are protected by copyright law so if you want to perform them, the first thing you'll need is a licence. This simple process helps support the playwright by ensuring they get paid for their work, and means that you'll have the documents you need to stage the show in public.

Not all our shows are available to perform all the time, so it's important to check and apply for a licence before you start rehearsals or commit to doing the show.

LEARN MORE & FIND THOUSANDS OF SHOWS

Browse our full range of plays and musicals and find out more about how to license a show
www.samuelfrench.co.uk/perform

Talk to the friendly experts in our Licensing team for advice on choosing a show, and help with licensing
plays@samuelfrench.co.uk   020 7387 9373

Acting Editions

BORN TO PERFORM

Playscripts designed from the ground up to work the way you do in rehearsal, performance and study

---

Larger, clearer text for easier reading

Wider margins for notes

Performance features such as character and props lists, sound and lighting cues, and more

---

+ CHOOSE A SIZE AND STYLE TO SUIT YOU

STANDARD EDITION

Our regular paperback book at our regular size

SPIRAL-BOUND EDITION

The same size as the Standard Edition, but with a sturdy, easy-to-fold, easy-to-hold spiral-bound spine

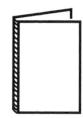

LARGE EDITION

A4 size and spiral bound, with larger text and a blank page for notes opposite every page of text. Perfect for technical and directing use

---

LEARN MORE | **samuelfrench.co.uk/actingeditions**

FIND PERFECT PLAYS TO PERFORM AT
www.samuelfrench.co.uk/perform

ABOUT THE AUTHORS

MATTHEW BALDWIN

Matthew Baldwin is a writer and actor.

In 2013 Matthew and his colleague Thomas Hescott developed *The Act*, for Ovalhouse. Matthew was nominated for an Off West End Award for Best Actor and jointly nominated with Thomas in the category of Most Promising Playwright. In 2014 *The Act* transferred to Trafalgar Studios in the West End with Matthew reprising his role.

Also in 2014 Matthew and Thomas wrote *Outings* for James Seabright Productions, which enjoyed a successful run at the Gilded Balloon for the Edinburgh Fringe Festival and subsequently a national tour and into the West End.

In 2017 he was named on the BBC's New Talent Hotlist.

Also in 2017 Matthew has written *I Miss the War*, part of the eight part series *Queers*, for BBC Four, starring Ian Gelder and directed by Mark Gatiss. This work was also be performed at the Old Vic.

THOMAS HESCOTT

Thomas is a writer and a director.

In 2017 he was named on the BBC's New Talent Hotlist.

Television credits (as director) include *EastEnders*.

He directed *The Dark Room* – a short film featuring David Mitchell, Miles Jupp and Matthew Baldwin. The film premiered at the 2016 London Short Film Festival.

Theatre credits include *The Act* for Ovalhouse (as co-writer and director). The production was nominated for two Off West End Theatre Awards, including Most Promising Playwright, and transferred to the West End. He also directed the recent West End production of *Tory Boyz* by James Graham.

Other credits as director include: *Wolves at the Window* (Arcola and Off-Broadway), *The British Ambassadors Belly Dancer* (Arcola and Arts Theatre, West End) and *Anatol* (Arcola), *Romeo and Juliet*, *Macbeth* and *Twelfth Night* (Southwark Playhouse), *Reunion* (Bridewell) and *Our Thing* (Gate).

AUTHORS' NOTE

As part of Ovalhouse Theatre's fiftieth anniversary celebrations they commissioned five plays to celebrate five decades of counterculture. *The Act* explored gay counterculture of the 1960s – the decade that led to the partial decriminalisation of male homosexual acts.

We'd both been very aware of generations of men who had been thrust into an underground world, not through choice but through necessity – some men embracing that world, and some finding it an uncomfortable fit. We were both aware of the rights that we often took for granted that had been hard won by those who came before. But we were also acutely aware of the prejudices, misogyny and class politics that were ever present within that world. *The Act* tries to capture that world in all its glory and with all its flaws. The protagonist, Matthews, is someone for whom the audience should feel empathy, but he's also a snob, and deeply flawed – the trick is to enjoy playing him and all his flaws. He isn't a saint.

The Act is a one-man play. The audience enjoys the seamless jumps from character to character – the acting athletics is part of the fun of the piece. Staging should be kept simple. In the original production we used sound to move us from location to location and to underscore the scenes. We embraced the old-fashioned radio plays of the day, using an old microphone for the narration.

When *The Act* transferred to Trafalgar Studios in the West End we were sought out by producer James Seabright to work with him on *Outings*. In 2014 there didn't seem to be a week that went by without some celebrity coming out. James and his general manager, Oli Seadon, had spotted this trend, and were aware of how coming out had changed over the decades. They commissioned us to create a play that told real life coming-out stories from around the world.

Outings was always intended to be performed by well-known actors, comedians and celebrities. All the stories, whilst not being strictly verbatim, are real life stories – some people submitted their stories to us via a website, some we met and interviewed, a few were people we knew already. We felt a great responsibility to represent their story as truthfully and as accurately as possible. If they're funny – it's because the person who told us the story found it funny (we all use humor with the darkest of experiences). If we're laughing in the performance, and we should be laughing, it is with the protagonist, not at them.

One of the hardest aspects of staging *Outings* is to understand that the action is about someone telling us a story – it is not about recreating that story. The "present tense" is speaker and listener in the same room. *Outings* doesn't work if you try and stage the stories fully – there are moments when other characters speak – they act as brief flashbacks – but the action of the play is someone telling someone else a story.

The original production had a rotating cast of performers, and is designed for four actors. We have kept the actor breakdown as it was originally, but there is nothing to stop a director using more actors, should they wish. When *Outings* was produced as a charity gala in the West End every story was read by a different celebrity – either way works.

Thomas Hescott and Matthew Baldwin
July 2017

MUSIC USE NOTE

Outings was produced by James Seabright Productions and opened at the Edinburgh Fringe Festival in August 2014. It subsequently toured the UK, and in 2017 came into the West End.

Outings was performed by a rotating cast including:

Tom Allen
Stephen K Amos
Adèle Anderson
Simon Callow
Scott Capurro
Jo Caulfield
Revd Richard Coles
Rob Crouch
Jim Davidson
Rob Deering
Andrew Doyle
Mark Farrelly
Jade Godley
Kerry Godliman
Russell Grant
Andrew Hayden-Smith

Julie Hesmondhalgh
Sharon Horgan
Luke Kempner
Shappi Khorsandi
Caroline Lennon
Nichola McAuliffe
Hardeep Singh Kohli
Margaret Thatcher – Queen of Soho
Zoe Lyons
Shazia Mirza
Adam Riches
Mark Thomas
Camille Ucan

Written by Thomas Hescott and Matthew Baldwin
Directed by David Grindley
Designed by Janet Bird
Lighting by Jason Taylor
Sound by Tom Lishman

The Act originally ran at Ovalhouse from 8th to 26th October 2013:

Company

Director and Writer – Thomas Hescott
Actor and Writer – Matthew Baldwin
Assistant Director – Jamie Jackson
Lighting Designer – Ed Locke
Illustrator – Gavin Dobson
Musician – Tim Saward

The Act subsequently transferred to Trafalgar Studios from 25th February to 29th March 2014.

Company

Director and Writer – Thomas Hescott
Actor and Writer – Matthew Baldwin
Assistant Director – Jamie Jackson
Lighting Designer – Ed Locke
Sound Designer – Rob Donnelly-Jackson
Illustrator – Gavin Dobson
Musician – Tim Saward
General Manager – Peter Huntley

ACKNOWLEDGEMENTS

We are grateful to Rebecca Atkinson-Lord and Rachel Briscoe for commissioning *The Act*, and for their support and notes as the play developed, and to everyone at Ovalhouse for their support with the production.

Thank you to Peter Lloyd for so much insight into the characters and the world of the play.

Thank you to Peter Huntley for spotting an opportunity and transferring the play into Trafalgar Studios.

Thank you to James Seabright for commissioning us to write *Outings*, thanks to our four core cast members – Camille, Andrew, Rob and Zoe – and our director David Grindley.

We are indebted to everyone who told us their coming-out stories – some of whom we have never met – thank you for trusting us to tell your stories.

Finally thank you to Dan Usztan – the best agent we could have.

For Dean and for Haydn

OUTINGS

CHARACTERS

Outings was originally written to be performed by four actors – two male and two female. This script has kept the character breakdown as it was originally performed; however there is no reason a director working with a larger company has to keep to this character breakdown. It is entirely possible for each story to be assigned to a different actor (as we did for the West End gala).

Where it seems useful, we have given the age and accent for the character. If casting each story separately, we would advise casting as close to type (in terms of age and nationality) as you can. Of course, with four actors this becomes less relevant.

ACTOR A: Male
How Would You Come Out
A Closet Story
A Nurse's Story
A Story About ME (20s)
Four Short Stories
A Story About Treatment (nurse)
A Story About Bruises (20s)
Things Gay People Are Asked
A Jehova's Witness's Story (20s)
A Trans Story
A Football Fan's Story (20s, Leicester)
A Story About A Yoghurt Spoon
A Drama Queen's Story (20s)

ACTOR B: Female
How Would You Come Out
Two Short Stories
A Nurse's Story (mother)
A Story About Running Away (young girl)
A Daughter's Story (20s)

Four Short Stories
Things Gay People Are Asked
A Trans Story (20s, pre-transition)
A Teacher's Story (primary-school girl)
An Immigrant's Story
A Story About A Note
A Christian Story (20s)

ACTOR C: Male
How Would You Come Out
Two Short Stories (Yorkshire)
A Story About ME (older brother of narrator)
A Daughter's Story (father of a girl in her 20s)
Four Short Stories
A Story About Treatment (60s, Liverpool)
A Mother's Story (son of narrator, American)
A Trans Story (father of narrator)
A Teacher's Story (Scottish)
A Story About A Funeral
An NGO's Story (Nepali taxi driver)
An Airman's Story
A Christian Story (preacher)

ACTOR D: Female
How Would You Come Out
Two Short Stories (mother of narrator, Yorkshire)
A Story About Running Away
Four Short Stories
A Wife's Story
A Story About Treatment (narrator's mother)
A Mother's Story (American)
Things Gay People Are Asked
A Trans Story (mother of narrator)
An NGO's Story
A Story About A Yoghurt Spoon (mum of narrator)
An Immigrant's Story (Zimbabwe)
A Drama Queen's Story (mother of narrator)

There are no specific lighting and sound cues. The original production had no props – with guests reading the stories.

SCENES

ACT ONE

HOW WOULD YOU COME OUT?
A CLOSET STORY
TWO SHORT STORIES
A NURSE'S STORY
A STORY ABOUT RUNNING AWAY
A STORY ABOUT ME
A DAUGHTER'S STORY
FOUR SHORT STORIES
A WIFE'S STORY
A STORY ABOUT TREATMENT
A STORY ABOUT BRUISES
A MOTHER'S STORY

ACT TWO

THINGS GAY PEOPLE ARE ASKED
A JEHOVA'S WITNESS'S STORY
A TRANS STORY
A TEACHER'S STORY
A FOOTBALL FAN'S STORY
A STORY ABOUT A FUNERAL
AN NGO'S STORY
A STORY ABOUT A YOGHURT SPOON
AN IMMIGRANT'S STORY
AN AIRMAN'S STORY
A STORY ABOUT A NOTE
A DRAMA QUEEN'S STORY
A CHRISTIAN STORY

ACT ONE

How Would You Come Out?

ACTOR D How do people come out? Have you come out? How would you do it?

ACTOR A We set ourselves a task last year. To gather as many coming out stories as we could. From as many countries as we could, from as many generations as we could.

ACTOR C We asked people on the web, we found websites devoted to coming-out stories, we asked people on Twitter, we travelled around recording our conversations wherever we went.

ACTOR B We collected over one hundred stories. Some happy, some sad, some silly. People would often say...

ACTOR A Me? Oh my story is totally boring.

ACTOR D Before they told us something beautiful, personal and unique.

ACTOR A Wherever we went we asked the same questions. Old or young, wherever we were, the questions were the same, even if the answers weren't. We'd ask...

ACTOR C When did you know?

ACTOR D I guess I was seven.

ACTOR A I was eleven.

ACTOR C Nine.

ACTOR B Thirty-four.

ACTOR C There were some boys on the school bus. They were older than me. At night I imagined them getting it on with girls. I gradually realized I was more into them than the girls they were with.

ACTOR A I joined the Cub Scouts to be around the other boys. I was seven.

ACTOR C Four years old. Nothing taught me.

ACTOR D My church equated gayness with selfish hedonism. I didn't feel like that so I didn't realize I was gay. At first.

ACTOR C I'd just discovered euroboy.com. That's where I found out there was a word for how I felt – that it was called gay.

ACTOR B I saw Lynda Carter as Wonder Woman and that was it for me.

ACTOR A I saw John Craven on *Newsround* and that was it for me.

ACTOR C I was about eleven or twelve I guess. I would get crushes on certain male friends. It would get extremely awkward.

ACTOR A The moment that I remember most was when I was twelve, and this boy and I were insulting each other and he said, "Well at least I'm not gay like you." And I thought, "You're right, I am."

ACTOR D I watched this girl from my class when I was thirteen dancing at my friend's bat mitzvah. I had a crush on her for the rest of the year.

ACTOR C I was doing homework on Henry VIII. I read that he was "a very handsome man in his youth", a "hunk". Curious, I googled "hunk" and what I found I liked. Very much.

ACTOR A I didn't realize two boys could be together. I thought that if I wanted to be with a boy, I'd have to become a girl. So at age four or five I was convinced I'd grow up, become a girl, and fall in love with a boy.

ACTOR B 1996. I was eight at a wedding reception. There was this girl in her teens and when I saw her, I felt the strongest, most intense butterflies, for the first time. I couldn't stop looking at her. She had big, blue, mysterious eyes, flowing chocolate-coloured hair, and just the most alluring smile I had ever seen. I didn't talk to her, I never found out who she was and I never asked. Never saw her again.

A Closet Story

ACTOR A I've known I was gay since I was eleven but have always found it hard to talk about. It's not really because I'm gay, it's because I have never been happy with the way I look.

When I was at school I was bullied and it wasn't until my final year that I actually started to stick up for myself, but by then I had no self-confidence at all and I weighed eighteen stone. I'm still battling with my weight now and I am convinced that because I am a larger guy no one will love me.

When I was thirteen I had my first gay experience; it was with my only friend in middle school. I went to his house one Saturday and we got bored so I asked if he wanted to play poker. My friend said yes but we didn't know what we could bet so I suggested our clothes. It was the most exciting time of my life, especially because his parents were downstairs. After we both lost our clothes he suggested we experiment a little.

Over the next few years we did more and he came out to his parents, but I never. I was scared of their reaction. Also, I felt like I was disappointing them.

I've always kept people at a distance. I have come out to friends before and have been told that I will burn in hell. I always seem to worry too much what other people think and expect of me. Although I love my family, I don't want to upset them. I feel that looking the way I do, when I do tell them and if they don't accept me, then I'll be on my own with nobody in my life and nowhere to live.

I have two brothers, who each have four kids, but I still want kids of my own. I love my nieces and nephews and don't want my brothers to stop me seeing them. Why is this so hard?

It's like there are two versions of me; the one I let people see and the one I *want* them to see.

Does that make sense?

I know that this is meant to be about coming out and being OK with yourself, but how can you do that if, when you look in the mirror, you don't like what you see?

Two Short Stories

ACTOR C I was seeing a guy when I was seventeen. He was twenty-seven and a trollop! My naivety plus his promiscuity made it very difficult. We'd tried to patch things up with a soggy weekend in a tent near Scarborough.

When I got back I was having a bit of a weep in my bedroom. My mother came into my room and asked what was wrong, I didn't tell her so she told me.

ACTOR D You're involved with that Ian aren't you?

ACTOR C I burst into tears, but managed a small "yes", to which *she* replied—

ACTOR D I just can't bear to wash your pants anymore!

ACTOR B It was the summer before I went to university, and I felt like I really needed to tell my dad before I left. He's a doctor, and he always had conversations with me about contraception and birth control. We were on a bike ride and the pressure for me to come out was building.

ACTOR C (DAD) So make sure you use a condom, y'know, you don't want to be getting pregnant at university.

ACTOR B That won't be a problem, 'cause I'm gay.

It just slipped out! I hadn't planned on saying anything that day! I nearly fell off my bloody bike in the shock of it.

There was a moment of awkward silence.

ACTOR C Well.

That could change.

ACTOR B And that was it! He just changed the subject!

A Nurse's Story

ACTOR A So at school one day our homework was to get our parents to write down what they expected from us when we got older, what and who they wanted us to be, which was to be sealed and not opened until the teacher read them out in class. My mum loved being involved with stuff, and so jumped at the chance of writing down exactly what she expected from me. Did she want me to be a scientist? A doctor? A builder? A banker? Hell, a binman? The moment came to find out...

ACTOR B (MUM) I have no expectations other than to follow his dreams, his heart, his desires. Whether gay or straight, no matter what career he chooses, who he chooses to be or who he chooses to be with, I will be proud of him as I already am.

ACTOR A I could feel the eyes of the other kids boring holes deep into me wondering... Is he gay then?

Growing up, I never felt the need to come out to anyone. I never once felt that who I was was any different to who my mum or my dad were. I never once thought "I'm hiding a huge secret here, this will be a shock, I'm different to my siblings". So I didn't feel the need to come out. Well, not until the moment my mum first mentioned it.

I'm a nurse (of course I am) I was busily trying to eat in a quick lunch break, with my workmates, and the phone goes. I answer it hands free because I was trying to eat, and trying to sort paperwork at the same time, so I put my mum on speakerphone. The conversation was about me not having been home for a few nights and was everything ok, was I safe, etc.

ACTOR B So when do we get to meet this guy, I'm assuming he is your boyfriend because of how much time you spend there now? If you bring him over, it gives me a reason to get my hair done and cook a nice meal!

ACTOR A Bam. There it was. The first mention between us of me being gay, and my official outing to the world, without any help from myself.

Mum ...can I call you later?

ACTOR B (**MUM** *starts to break down, to cry*) Well, just let me know when you can bring him round and then I'll get my hair done. 'Cause you know it's not an issue, don't you? It's completely nothing to even think about with us, right?

ACTOR A Mum, I'm taking you off speakerphone. Why are you crying? You said it was OK?

ACTOR B I feel I must be a bad mother because you couldn't have told me earlier! I've known all your life, and I've tried to show it doesn't matter...to me, to us, but you couldn't tell me! I must have handled it wrong!

ACTOR A No, Mum, don't you see? It's because you handled it right that I had nothing to tell you. I feel no different to anyone else because of you. You couldn't have taught me better.

A Story About Running Away

ACTOR D It's my wedding day. I'm crying. Crying because I know I don't love my new husband.

At night, when I am in bed with my husband, Doug, I lie there next to him and think of Jo.

Jo was a girl I'd met at university. My parents had helped me move down to London and into the halls of residence. While my parents were still saying their goodbyes, a girl popped her head into the room and said hello.

From that moment, my whole life seemed to shift on its axis.

Jo and I became firm friends and within the first few days she told me she was gay. I was nineteen and I had never knowingly met a gay woman. Initially I was intrigued and found myself seeking her out at every opportunity. The more I saw her, the more I wanted to see her. She was like a drug to me. When Jo walked into a room, it lit up. Gradually I started to question how I felt about her.

It began to dawn on me that my feelings were far from platonic. At last I confessed how I was feeling. I think I shocked Jo at the time, as she saw me as her straight friend. Jo had a girlfriend back at home, although the relationship was pretty rocky. I started my personal campaign to win her over and eventually it paid off. The first time I slept with Jo, it was the scariest and yet the most mind-blowing experience. It switched something on inside me and that was it, I was totally hooked.

We went out with each other for three years. At this time I went through a bit of an identity crisis. I thought that if I was gay then I needed to look a certain way, so I cut all my hair off and tried to butch up. That was when I began to develop an incredible fear that my parents would find out.

When things ended with Jo, I went headlong into a mission to recreate myself. I ditched all my old friends and found new friends – ones who didn't know about my relationship. And that's when I met my husband.

Of course things end with Doug, we have three children but we can't make the marriage work. We get divorced.

I'm in a local gay bar having a drink with some friends when in walks the most beautiful woman I have ever seen. She is with a couple of friends. I can't work out if she is with either of them. We start talking and hit it off right away. The relationship quickly progresses. Within three weeks I know I am totally head over heels in love with her. I've never felt this way about anyone before, not even Jo. I decide the time has come to tell the children. They're seven, five and three. They just seem to accept that Mummy is in love with a woman.

My eldest turned rounds and says—

ACTOR B (DAUGHTER) Oh my God, my mummy is gay, how cool is that.

ACTOR D Telling my parents is a whole different experience. My mum cries down the phone and my dad refuses to speak to me. My mum keeps on going on about how I am a liar and asking how I can do this to her. My dad makes it clear he never wants to meet Sarah, my girlfriend. He tells me he doesn't want to meet her because he doesn't want to like her.

That was back in 2001. And over time my father softened, and they ended up getting on really well. Before he died he said that he saw her as his daughter-in-law. That meant so much.

My only regret is that it took me so long to realise that I couldn't run away from who I am. Coincidentally our eldest daughter has recently come out as gay at the age of nineteen. Thankfully her coming out story was a lot more straightforward. It went something like this—

ACTOR B Mum, I've got something to tell you... I think I'm gay and I've met this great girl.

ACTOR D Oh that's wonderful sweetheart, I'm really happy for you.

A Story About Me

ACTOR A And as I was lying on the operating table I thought, "if I die now no one will really know who I am."

I've had excess skin tissue removed from my chest, stomach, ribcage, back, buttocks and my legs.

And I've had to have pockets of fat removed and my belly button and my nipples removed.

I've had about 20 per cent of my skin cut off.

You see when I was eleven I developed ME, which I had for seven years that stopped...anything...social life, friends anything. I recovered when I was eighteen, but I had ballooned massively. I was fat. So I then had to go on a diet and lose nine stone. But that left me very badly disfigured by all the excess skin tissue.

So I've spent the last ten years having reconstructive surgery.

I was fifteen when I realized – I'd felt very shut off for a long time, and then we got the Internet. That's when I realized I was gay. I'd been stuck in my bedroom for years and I was like, "At last, finally I can see a bit of the world." And I ended up seeing some of the wrong things, if you know what I mean? I was feeling very isolated. It was another thing that made me feel different to everyone else.

My first piece of reconstructive surgery was when I was twenty. I didn't really realize the seriousness of the operation and I went to a local private clinic, and ended up having a very serious post-op complication. A bleed. And I woke up from the surgery to be told I was bleeding very badly and we need to take you back down to theatre.

The last thing I said to the anaesthetist was, "Please don't let me die."

As I came out of it, as I came round, still alive, I thought to myself, "I could be dead."

But lying there, I also thought – if I had died there on the operating table, no one would have really known me, no one would have known who I was. But it wasn't that which shocked me. It was the thought that that would have been better, the easier option. It shocked me that I thought that badly about myself.

I knew I had more surgery coming up (this time with the NHS!) and I couldn't risk that happening again, I couldn't risk dying with people not knowing who I was.

The first person I told was my biggest, scariest brother. He's much older than me, a builder, a real lad's lad, and I idolized him growing up. I was sitting on his sofa and it just came out.

I think I'm gay.

ACTOR C (**BROTHER**) You *think* you're gay?

ACTOR A No – I *know* I'm gay.

ACTOR C Well that's fine by me.

ACTOR A And I just sat there for a little while – it wasn't the reaction I'd expected. And I thought – OK well this is alright then.

ACTOR C Just don't come round here in a dress, alright?

ACTOR A It was all remarkably easy after all that.

A Daughter's Story

ACTOR B I can't quite remember when it finally happened. But I know it was 2001, and I'm pretty confident it was July, or maybe August. We were driving in the car.

Dad had been acting a little strange all day, and now it became clear why.

In a lull in conversation, he took a deep breath and began a prepared spiel.

ACTOR C I did this with your brother when he turned eighteen and now you are eighteen, and so I have put it off as much as I can.

ACTOR B He paused, staring straight ahead, focused on the traffic.

ACTOR C I have always promised myself that when you turned eighteen, I would give you the chance to ask me any question you liked and I would give you a completely honest answer.

ACTOR B Dad loved to have important conversations in the car. We'd had the sex talk in the car. We'd talked about sick family members, broken friendships, possible career changes involving relocating, my first boyfriend.

The car was for the big talks.

It was also where, as a small child, I would pretend to be asleep late at night when there was more than one adult in the car, just in case they ever said anything interesting.

They usually did.

And so I knew then, with one hundred percent certainty, where this conversation was going. My dad, who had split from my mother when I was very young, who always had male friends, who had always, as far as I could see, always been gay, my dad was now going to come out to me. I wasn't quite sure how we were going to get there, but I knew where we were headed.

ACTOR C Well? Don't you have any questions?

ACTOR B Dad was very tense. No, no, I don't think so.

ACTOR C Nothing?

ACTOR B The silence stretched between us. So I decided to bluff him out.

Well, there is *one* thing.

ACTOR C Yes?

ACTOR B He was eager, anxious.

When we were little and you would give us food and you wouldn't tell us what was in it...

ACTOR C Yes?

ACTOR B What was in it?

ACTOR C Seriously? You want to know what was in your dinner? I just don't think that's relevant.

ACTOR B Too bad, you said *anything*. Answer the question.

We drove along for a bit, Dad thinking where to go.

ACTOR C You really want to use your question on this?

ACTOR B Yes.

ACTOR C Right. Well, there was kidney, and there was the bits of the chicken you don't like, and once... there was duck.

ACTOR B I was appalled.

DUCK! You fed me duck?!

ACTOR C Yes. You had no idea.

ACTOR B I can't believe you would do that.

ACTOR C Sorry.

ACTOR B I don't know when I developed the attachment, but for as long as I can remember ducks have been my favourite animals. I think maybe it had something to do with Jemima Puddleduck.

For my entire life I have avoided eating them, I just couldn't do it. But there it was. The man had fed me Jemima Puddleduck, and told me she was chicken.

I bristled a little and was momentarily distracted from the real problem at hand.

There was silence in the car again as we inched past the car yards that signalled our neighbourhood is not far off.

ACTOR C So that's your only question?

ACTOR B Yes, I think so.

But I think there's something that you want to tell me, and I know what it is, and I truly believe it's not my place to ask you, it's your place to tell me – when you're ready.

ACTOR C How do I know I'm telling you the right thing?

ACTOR B Just say it, Dad.

And then he did. He told me all of it, and he made the pieces fit. The parts of our life that had made less sense to me as a small child. The moving, the housemates, the adults we were taught to love and treat as family, and who treated us that way.

He was annoyed, I think, that I had known the truth for some time, and had not said a word. But I never thought I had the right to question him, because he'd obviously made a choice not to tell me, and so I had respected that.

Besides, it never meant anything to me. It made no discernible difference. I can't remember feeling differently about him after I'd figured it out. Years ago.

He was just Dad. He gave me love and safety and security. He taught me perseverance and how to argue and when to argue. He loved me, and trusted me, and I knew from the get-go it was unconditional. I guess I'd always just felt that love was a two-way street. I owed it to him too.

He looked at me, mischief in his eyes. Took a deep breath.

ACTOR C Your brother had no idea.

ACTOR B I was amazed. My brother is the smartest person I know. How could he have not known? Dad never hid anything; the men he loved he loved with his whole heart and he shared them with us. We used to get into bed with Dad and his partner when we were little; we would make Dad Father's Day breakfasts with his partner. We holidayed together, as a family. They slept together, held hands, kissed, touched each other in that way lovers do. Not with jazz hands, but discreetly. Dad never pretended to us that he was *not* in love with those men.

Another pause.

Why didn't you just tell me?

ACTOR C I didn't know... I didn't want to ruin anything. I didn't want to disappoint you... I was worried you wouldn't love me anymore.

ACTOR B His shoulders, big, strong Dad shoulders, were heaving.

Dad. Do you love me?

ACTOR C Yes.

ACTOR B Do you love my brother?

ACTOR C Yes, of course.

ACTOR B Well, what the fuck do I care who else you love?

In that moment I was angry. Not at him, not at all. I was angry at the world, at his life, at the way that he had been made to feel all these years. That this man, who I know would do anything for me, would give his life for mine, would not even flinch at it, would feel such shame at who he is. That he would entertain for even a second that his children might feel that shame too.

It is an ugly realization, that your parents are fallible. It is a whole other thing to find out that they might worry your love for them is too.

Four Short Stories

ACTOR D It was the eve of the millennium. I didn't have the courage to face my sister face to face, so I called her to say I'm gay. I didn't want to enter a new century without my family knowing.

ACTOR C I hadn't planned to do it. I'd thought about it, I could see it happen. It's the National School's Public Speaking Competition and I'm speaking in front of the whole school and I just said it. It just came out, "I'm gay."

ACTOR B When I came out to my dad he was relieved, he thought I was going to ask him for money.

ACTOR A It did help that when I told my father I was bisexual he said he was too.

A Wife's Story

ACTOR D Forget closets. The place where gay men hide with the women they married is in the cupboard under the stairs. This is the dark space where we keep those things we want unseen by the rest of the world. Her friends and family don't see what's in there, in fact, it's probably best if they don't. Explaining to them what is in the cupboard is just too hard: she doesn't have the right words to say it, and they don't have the experience to hear it. They can't understand this. The woman has a home, and because she loves her home, she wants to keep it just the way it is. She accidentally married a gay man and so she lives in her cupboard under the stairs.

Home is her comfort and salve, the retreat when the rest of the world is too cold, too unfriendly, too busy, too quiet. It's where she knows where the tin foil is, and that the upstairs bedroom door slams when the back door is open, and where the carpet is loose on the fifth rise, and where the single, simple act of putting a key in a lock is a single, simple act of breathing in.

It's where the people she loves live all the time, or sometimes. The pillows smell of their hair, their shoes sit by the front door refusing to run themselves upstairs, their pictures smile in their frames, their finger prints smear the bathroom mirror and an odd sock waits patiently in the washing basket for its partner to be found under the bed.

She's gone into hiding in the cupboard under her stairs to keep her home safe, and she shuts the door. He tells her what the marriage means: the two people who love each other most in the world stay married, but the gay one gets to have sex with anyone they want, and the wife chooses to go along with it. Clearly for him the benefits are considerable: he gets to have his cake; he gets to eat his cake. But in the dark, she can't be sure what her benefits are.

The woman does a lot of thinking in the cupboard under the stairs. She has known for many years that the tiny words "us" and "we" have always meant her and him, that while she struggles to find the words to describe her life, she uses the words "us" and "we" as shorthand for all their shared experiences, to convey to the rest of the world that they are a couple, that they know each other, understand what the presence or the absence of a look, a touch, a word or a quietness means. But one day her husband used those words, "us" and "we", when talking about another. He didn't even notice it. He didn't mean to hurt her, but in that moment she knew how painful and powerful those words could be. The intimacy that once existed between them has gone, because intimacy simply can't be shared.

He doesn't notice that as he walks through the door, he brings with him an unfamiliar smell. This isn't the smell of sex – it's the smell of other, it is the smell of someone else's home, where the man she loves has lain on another's bed and left his smell on another's pillow. In this cupboard, he says that this is the best way, that this means he won't be promiscuous, that he will have a "monogamous" relationship with one man, who in turn, is faithful to him. He will say, "This isn't about love, it's just about sex." And this is her unbearable paradox: she should feel reassured that she is still loved, but hurt that he would do this to her, for someone he doesn't love.

And then one day he says that he is "fond" of this other person, and suddenly she longs for it not to be love. He has begun something new and exciting: he can't wait to get ready, to go out, to be wanted, to want, to be thrilled, to be alive, but none of these feelings are for her.

She comforts him in his transition because he's her best friend, and yet she hates him, and wants to find some punishment through her words and actions that will show him how much she is hurt. She feels bloodied and scarred but there are no wounds for anyone to see. They spend hours under the stairs negotiating the rules. They agree not to talk about when he is going out and when he will be back, and then after an interminable month she demands to know when he is going out and when he'll be back. She knows that nothing she can say, do, wear, lose, gain, embellish, reduce will make any difference but she tries them all. She needs to know that it wasn't all a mirage, that once she was loved and wanted.

She knows one day he will fall in love, and he'll want more. He has already begun to move away from what was. He can't stay in the cupboard under the stairs because there is just too much going on outside. He begins to bend the rules, he begins to justify what he does, he begins to open the door and let the light in.

And then, it's not just him who comes out. Her friends are curious, scandalized, shocked, unsurprised. They tell her they knew what she didn't, that she was deluded because she couldn't see what was obvious to them. They know her home you see, and they think they know all the dark places. They don't. They talk about how hard it must have been for him and she agrees, because this isn't about her. She feels unloved, unattractive, undesirable, a failure, stupid and exposed. She sees his life begin, and hers end. She no longer cares about preserving her home. She forgets where the loose carpet is on the stair and her feet slide out from under her, and there is no longer anything to catch hold of. It's been hard to leave the cupboard, because although it's dark, at least she knew she was in there with him. She chose, at all costs, to make it a place of comfort, to be at home with the spiders and the wellingtons and the Christmas decorations. But once the door opened, her choice to stay was taken away. She has to leave, and find somewhere new.

And then one day she does. In her new home, she knows when to duck when she comes down the stairs and she knows where the tin foil is. It is still a place where people that love her come, and they still smile from their frames, and they still leave their fingerprints on the mirror. But now the single, simple act of putting the key in the door is a single, simple act of breathing out, and in this home, there is no cupboard under the stairs.

The Story About Treatment

ACTOR C (LIVERPUDLIAN) 1958.

I couldn't make out what it was about. I knew the lads would mess about in the Scouts but I seemed to enjoy it *more* than them. They seemed to grow away from it and I didn't. So at the age of twelve I went to my doctor.

I went to my doctor and said, "I'm a homosexual", because the word "gay" didn't exist. And he laughed in my face and told me to get out.

I went back at fourteen and he proscribed lithium, I think it was. I threw them down the toilet. A fourteen-year-old boy. I thought, "I'm not taking any tablets, I can't change who I am, I thought he was going to help me." So I put them down the toilet.

From fourteen to eighteen I fought it and fought it.

1964.

I used to save up days from work so I could go to London and be myself. So I would jump on the train. I was seventeen/eighteen. I would get to London, coat over my shoulder, cigarette holder out, drinking gin and tonics, and I minced. I was trying to find who I was. I was the campest thing on two legs – I didn't think anyone knew. I was in hotpants on the front page of the *Daily Gazette*. I was bizarrely camp. And I thought nobody could see.

I lived at home with my mother. I was adopted and I worshiped my mother because she gave me everything. She was my life. My mother found a letter, and it was one of those letters which was ridiculous silly stuff, but I kept it. And it fell out of my desk and my mother found it. I came home from work, from the Cabin Club - it was about 2am in the morning. She was sitting up in bed, looking like death. She looked like death. I said, "What's wrong?

ACTOR D (MUM) What's this?

ACTOR C And it was the letter.

I said, "Mum. I'm a homosexual."

To which she promptly vomited.

She loved me with a passion, but she'd had a bad marriage so she was anti sex. There was a lot not going for her.

She cried herself to sleep for the next three years. Every night for three years. She didn't want me to have the pain. In those days, all my gay friends were married – that's what you did.

ACTOR D I want you to go to a doctor's.

ACTOR C I told her I'd been before. She was horrified.

The doctor told me there was a cure. And I knew by this time there wasn't a cure, but the doctor said there was and I was doing this for Mum. And she was in a terrible state, so I said, yes – I'd go for the cure.

So I went to the hospital. It's still there, not the block I went to, that's been pulled down, but the hospital is still there. It was a psychiatric ward. No, it wasn't – it was a loony bin.

I was scared shitless. I was eighteen going on nineteen. A boy. Not knowing what was going to happen to me. I changed my name because it was a criminal offence. So I was in there, locked up and nobody knew I was there. Nobody knew I was there or who I was. The overriding feeling the whole time was I've got to get out of here alive.

I'll always remember they had a TK20 Grundy tape recorder and they asked me what I did sexually, and it was brutal, and about degrading you. And that lasted an hour.

And then they put me in a room, and they asked me what I drank. Well, I drank Guinness. And so I went into this room and there were crates of Guinness and dirty books, which in those days were pictures of men in bathing costumes up to their chest.

There was a male nurse over there, the tape recorder there, and there's the booze. So I'm in the room, drinking the booze, looking at the books and after some time they gave

me an injection that made me feel violently ill. Both ends...
So. I said, "I think I'm gonna be..."

And they said—

ACTOR A (NURSE) Just do it there.

ACTOR C So I was sick in the bed.

That lasted an hour.

And an hour.

And an hour.

Seventy-two hours. Without one break. Without any food.
Without anything at all.

They tortured me.

My arm looked like I was a drug addict.

I was absolutely demented. Demented.

So much so, I thought, "Will I ever get out of here alive?"
That's all I was bothered about.

I said, "I volunteered – I am here voluntarily and I've had
enough".

I said, "I – Want – Out."

They wanted to put electrodes on to my penis next.

"I – Want – Out."

I was like a raving lunatic.

And I stormed out. I don't know if I was allowed to leave,
but I did, I stormed out.

When I got home, I lay in a bath of water for eight hours.

My mother never forgave me. But I never told her what they
did. Because if I'd told her what they did I hate to think. She
would have topped herself, she would have gone ballistic at
what they'd done to me. So she died not knowing.

But now – I live in a mainstream world. My radio show
has one million listeners, and I don't want to be known as
a "Gay DJ", I want to be known as "The Best" DJ. I don't
want to be ghettoized. I don't want to live in a ghetto. And

I get very cross with young gay guys, with their rejection of old gay men. Because we gave them everything, we fought for everything and they forgot that.

A Story About Bruises

ACTOR A It's the bruises. The bruises that out me.

I'm fourteen years old. I don't feel close to either of my parents. Or anyone. I was bullied in school for being different. I was very short and small. At school the worst thing is to be called gay. I had rubbers thrown at me constantly. Other kids would flick me with rulers as I walked past. It sounds silly now but it takes its toll. Every single day. For years. Gay, gay, gay. I once sang a song in assembly. Some boys recorded it and played it back to me every day afterwards. Gay. Every day for years being told that I was the worst thing in the world. I felt like something was missing, I didn't feel loved by anyone.

My dad used to coach football locally and my two brothers went there too. One day I went there with my dad and his mates said, "Who's this?" and he said, "My middle son". "I didn't know you had a middle son", his friend said. That really hurt me. He wasn't proud enough of me to even tell them I was alive. I didn't get on with my mother much either. I knew how both my parents felt about gays and I was petrified they would find out.

So I'm fourteen and lonely. I can't come out. So I talk to people on the Internet, as loserish as it sounds. I felt like it was the only outlet where I could meet and speak to like-minded people. I started speaking to one guy. He was in the army. Twenty, muscly, handsome. Not a dirty old man or anything. He drew me in with promises of love and friendship and all that shit, and I fell for it.

It was a really strange part of my life, I let it happen because I didn't feel I had anyone else, he was 100 per cent in control of every aspect of my life. I was weak and depressed. I didn't feel like I had much to live for. He ended up abusing me, physically, sexually and emotionally. He raped me many times. I kid you not, he even faked a suicide over a web cam while I listened. He told me it was because I didn't love him enough, I wasn't giving him what he needed. He was talking about killing himself and then the cam went off but the sound stayed on and there was a big bang and then the sound of people screaming. I believed he had killed himself because of me. I was distraught, inconsolable, traumatized. The day after it had happened, he came back online, telling me it was a test to see how much I loved him.

My mother could see something was wrong but I felt like she was afraid of asking questions in case she'd get answers she didn't want to hear.

It was the bruises that gave me away. The bruises that outed me. I used to say that I was staying at my friend's house and I once came back covered in bruises and she thought it was my friend, and I couldn't let her think that, so I said, "I'm seeing someone, and it *is* what you think, I am gay". She told me I should call Childline. I needed to talk to her and she completely flew off the handle. "DON'T TELL YOUR DAD. If you tell your dad while you're still under his roof it will be bad."

After everything that had happened to me, then talking to her, it was like kicking a dog when it's down.

I was terrified for years that I had AIDS. Protection was never on the cards with him. Sometimes he raped me more than once in a night.

My mother still doesn't know what happened to me, or the events that happened in that horrific year. I'm twenty-two now and, if I'm honest, I always felt ashamed of what happened to me so I rarely told anyone. Rape and sexual abuse is something that we as a society rarely recognize happens to males, but it does, and teenage gay males like I was, who can't come out, can be vulnerable. I bet there are boys just like I was, looking for a means to an end, and trusting the wrong people.

A Mother's Story

ACTOR D When did I know?

I guess I began to realize my son was gay when he was sixteen. His stepdad and I talked about this gut feeling of mine, and we worried about how long it would take Erik to tell us, and how difficult it would be for him.

We were both acutely aware of what my sister, Jill, had gone through. She is now among those in California making plans to exercise her new marriage rights, but she didn't come out until she was in her mid-thirties. She brought the whole family together in her therapist's office to share what had long been a *shameful secret* in her life.

I was determined my son would not go through the same shame. But I didn't want to push him, either. If he was, indeed, gay, it was up to him to decide who to tell and when. So I waited. I tried to help by giving him signs. I championed gay rights whenever I could. And finally, on a December afternoon during a break from college, Erik gave me the best gift I will ever receive. It was this letter...

ACTOR C Dear Mom,

You asked me to give you a letter for Christmas. Thank you for asking. The moment you asked, I knew what I wanted to say.

I want to be more open and straightforward with you. I want to be able to communicate with you to the fullest extent possible and not have any secrets.

There's a conversation that you've been trying to have with me for a long time. I've seen you try to start it and then I've shut you out and ended the conversation as quickly as possible. I've been a brick wall of silence. I'm sorry for that.

I've begun this letter before, but never finished it. I once dreamt that I wrote it and in my dream, I was extremely eloquent – but then I woke up and I couldn't remember the words.

Every time you've tried to start this conversation, I've been afraid to continue it. I don't know why I'm afraid. It's just a difficult conversation to begin. So here goes, I'm going to begin it now: I love you, I'm gay, let's talk.

Love, Erik.

ACTOR D After I read the letter, we cried, hugged and finally had that talk I'd been hoping for since he was sixteen.

But why didn't he tell me sooner?

ACTOR C I knew my incredibly supportive family would be OK with it. The problem was, I wasn't OK with it. When I was a kid, the most common playground insults were "you're so gay" and "faggot". Every time I heard those words, they stung. Because even if those words weren't aimed at me, they still landed on me. They taught me at a young age that being gay was a bad thing, worthy of ridicule. It was the worst insult you could sling at someone. I learned to police my behaviour: don't speak in certain ways, don't dress in certain ways, don't do anything to give yourself away, don't let anyone know *you're* the thing they make fun of.

I grew out of that, thank God, and embraced myself, and came out, but every time I hear about another young gay kid killing himself after getting bullied, my heart aches because I know what that kid went through. Why does the word "faggot" still have such an impact on playgrounds? Why do the bullies still have the power to make "gay" a put-down, to make homosexuality worthy of hate and ridicule?

ACTOR D And here's another question: why does it still have to be such a big deal when someone in the public eye comes out? NBA player Jason Collins made international headlines when he became the first openly gay man in a major American professional sport. It's time to stop keeping track of firsts like this. Jason wrote in *Sports Illustrated*: "I wish I wasn't the kid in the classroom raising his hand and saying, 'I'm different.' If I had my way, someone else would have already done this. Nobody has, which is why I'm raising my hand."

Each hand that gets raised makes it easier for the next one to go up.

And to make it easier for people like Jason, we all need to raise our hands.

My son has promised me grandchildren. I want them to grow up in a world in which no one needs to make announcements about their sexual orientation.

Right after I read his Christmas letter, I said, "I'm so grateful that you were finally able to tell me who you are."

Erik gently corrected me:

ACTOR C No, Mom, this isn't who I am, any more than being heterosexual is who you are. It's like having blue or brown eyes. It's the way you're born. It just is.

ACT TWO

Things Gay People Are Asked

ACTOR A Things gay people are asked—

ACTOR D You're gay?

ACTOR C Is that why you dress so well?

ACTOR B Do you fancy me?

ACTOR D How do you know it's not a phase?

ACTOR C Are you the man or the woman?

ACTOR A Why do some lesbians like girls who look like guys?

ACTOR D Don't you want kids?

ACTOR C Does it hurt?

ACTOR A Do you get...you know...on your...?

ACTOR B How do you know you're not straight if you've never tried it?

ACTOR C Does your father know?

ACTOR D What do you actually do?

ACTOR A Can I watch?

ACTOR B What made you turn?

ACTOR C Do you just...? *(makes scissoring actions with hands)*

ACTOR D How can you not find guys hot?

ACTOR B Oh I know this gay guy – you'd totally love him.

ACTOR C Is that why you're anti-religion?

ACTOR A When's Eurovision?

ACTOR D So you're a vegetarian?

ACTOR C Does that make you bifocal?

ACTOR B You're gay? I thought you were just posh.

A Jehova's Witness's Story

ACTOR A We never had Christmas or birthdays growing up. We had a very strong sense of community though. Lots of stability. They are very friendly people. They'll get on with anyone until it's within their own community. It's extreme. Because they're with each other constantly it's like a brain-washing effect. It only clicked later on.

I didn't notice at school, but when I got to college I started mixing with different kinds of people. I was in the college production of *Grease*. Played Vince Fonteyn because I can't sing. I realized I was gay. I'm not that camp though. But I'm camper than my brother. I have an identical twin. I felt very guilty. It had clicked in my head but then I knew that it was wrong for people like me. Being gay was banned, forbidden.

So I arrive home from college one day and find my mum and dad's car in the drive, and my grandad's, and three other family friends we knew. I walk in through the back room and they're all sat there, round a table. And my sister.

My sister had got into my computer and found some "images" that shouldn't have been there. Even though the computer had a pile of clothes on top of it! She had found some – incriminating evidence. And then she had told my parents.

So at the age of seventeen I got home from college to find this "panel" sitting around our dinner table. They told me to sit down and showed me what they had discovered on my computer. They told me to explain myself. Two worlds collided. I explained that I was gay and that I was seeing someone. They gave me two options: to repent and deal with my issues, or leave the family home, never to return.

This was the offer. I had to decide then and there. A seventeen-year-old boy facing my mum, my dad, my granddad. I chose to leave.

My mum then brought down two bin liners of clothes and told me to get out. Literally don't darken my doorstep ever again. I left and went to my closest friend from college. I then came out to my friends and everyone else.

I haven't spoken to any of them from that day to this. Six years.

I had no money, no family and all my relationships had come crashing down in the space of an hour.

If you're a Jehova's Witness you're not considered fully fledged until you've been committed, when you're an adult. But I had been committed early. Because I was so good. My family were big in the community. My granddad was very high up. But because of that I had to face the full consequences of being "disfellowshipped". I could have repented and been treated like a black sheep but that's not what I wanted at all.

Having been brought up believing I was abhorrent and disgusting, I believe equality is not a gift to be given, it is the right of everyone – no matter who you are.

A Trans Story

ACTOR B   Well this isn't going to be straightforward with me.

I didn't know I had a problem or that anything was amiss with my body. Because I was quite feminine and in a girl's body, no one seemed to have a problem with that. So I didn't really notice anything. I noticed I didn't like certain aspects of my body but I just thought that everyone felt like that. I thought that the whole point of puberty is that it changed all that and that it magically made you into...whatever.

The first thing I noticed was sexuality. I first came out as a lesbian. Well I didn't come out – I was kind of outed. I fell in love with a girl at school. As I was in a female body, I presumed I was a lesbian.

Also, I fancied Madonna.

So we were in a relationship for like five years, from the age of thirteen to the age of seventeen.

I was banned from this girl's house by her parents. I think they suspected. But we had nowhere else to go. So she snuck me into her house, and snuck me into her bedroom whilst her parents were in a different room.

And as I was leaving the next day, I was like running holding my shoes and her mum must have looked out the window and saw me. So she phoned up my mum.

That's how I was outed as a lesbian.

I told my mum that they'd brought me up to believe that it doesn't matter if you're gay or straight or whatever, so you can't really tell me you now have a problem with that.

My mum was like, "Yeah, but we didn't know about you then!"

I leave school, move to London, and go on the gay scene, and assumed I was a lesbian... I was out, and...

Well then...

I kind of stopped fancying women.

I tried.

I'd just come out to everyone.

It had been a huge amount of effort.

And...now...now I just wasn't feeling it.

I went to all these gay bars.

And then I started fancying guys, and I was like, "oh no that's beyond inconvenient." But it wasn't even that simple because I didn't fancy straight guys, I was fancying the camp gay guys.

And I didn't want to be a woman with a man – I wanted to be a man with a man.

I started to wish I had a penis.

Then one day I said to my mum "I would really like to have an operation so I could have a flat chest."

It was her reaction to that that made me think maybe this wasn't a normal thing to say.

She clearly found it odd – but I just thought it would be a really good look.

But I hadn't thought I was trans – that wasn't really something I knew about.

I was drinking a lot. It's not why I drank. But the drinking helped to distract me. I wasn't feeling my feelings a lot of the time.

But I was starting to feel really uncomfortable in my own body, and resentful of all my male friends. I could see they were treating me differently to how they treated each other. I could see they perceived me as female.

So I went on the drag scene. My plan was in order to feel more comfortable I would dress as a drag queen, and people would perceive me as male. It worked for a bit, but I would have to go home and undress and I'd still be female.

It was only when I stopped drinking that I knew I had to do something. Without the alcohol to suppress the feelings every day was like, "Get me out of this body!" I started to realize this body was not for me. I started going to support groups, going to counselling and exploring my options.

And so I had to come out to my parents, again.

I was so stressed out. I was going out for a cigarette every few seconds. They clearly knew something was wrong.

So my dad was like—

ACTOR C I'm going up to bed, but if you've got something to discuss with your mum you know you can.

ACTOR B I think he thought it would be easier for me if he wasn't there.

"Mum. I think I'm in the wrong body."

Helpfully, my mum likes to watch late-night TV like *Sex Change Hospital*, so she was quite well informed.

She was quite good that night, she was like—

ACTOR D You know we'll always love you.

ACTOR B But she was freaked out. Especially at what to tell other people. Especially what to tell my dad. She made me keep it a secret from my dad. She said it would kill him.

The atmosphere, you could cut with a knife, it was awkward. My dad knew there was something going on and it made him unhappy that we were all so unhappy.

We decided I should write him a letter and my mum would give him the letter. That way she could explain and he could have the space to decide if he wanted to speak to me right away or not.

And he was really great.

He was like—

ACTOR C I'm sorry you had to feel like this, and of course it doesn't matter about me, it's what you want to do.

ACTOR B But his major concern was how to tell my grandmother. But she was even better about it than my dad.

Coming out, everyone was more worried about someone else, and that other person – they never cared that much.

I came out as a lesbian.

Then I started sleeping with gay men, I told my parents I wasn't a lesbian.

They thought I was lying.

I then came out as trans.

It was a confusing time for my parents.

I think telling them that after I transitioned I was going to present as a gay man who did drag was the least surprising bit for them.

It all finally made sense. To me at least.

With LGBT – I've always identified with the G more than the T. I don't really think of myself as trans, it was something I did, an operation I had. I'm just me, I'm just androgynous.

Transition to ACTOR A.

I think the twenty-year-old me would be very confused as to what happened. My goal back then...was to be a club king till I died...in a club. So the idea that I could reach thirty-six, that I could be in my right body and that I wouldn't be drinking and that I wanted to stay at home with a hot chocolate... I think I would have thought some miracle must have happened, something very freaky must have gone down there. Which I guess it did. I think I would have had a lot of hope from that because the reason I wanted to die on the club scene was because I couldn't function in real life, so to hear that I could be comfortable in my own body, I would have thought that was quite incredible.

A Teacher's Story

ACTOR C Well, it started with the lessons. We were doing anti-bullying at school. And my class, because they're a bit crazy at lunch time, after lunch they're all a bit hyped up so I sit them down and watch *Newsround*. *Newsround* was doing anti-bullying week this year and it was focused on anti-LGBT language. After *Newsround* we all go round in a circle –

"Is there anything to talk about?"

Some of the kids were like, "What's gay, what's lesbian?" and I thought, "Right, fair enough" so we chat, I sort of, just unpacked it a bit more.

So I said, "So, who has heard the word "gay" being used in school as like, an insult?" And four or five kids put their hands up and I thought, "Well that's not good." Eight years old.

I said, "OK well, hands up if you've heard it used outside of school", and every single child put their hand up. I was like, "Oh God." So then I asked, "Who thinks that being gay or lesbian is wrong or bad in some way?" and over half of the class put their hand up and I was like, "Oh crap!"

So the next day we did a lesson. It wasn't like we sat down and I said, "Right kids, I'm gay", it was, "Right, we're going to talk more about anti-bullying and language." We talked about the language that they heard and knew wasn't good, like "gay" and "poof" and "lesbian" as things that were bad.

So I was like, "OK, well what are these things?" And we did this bit on stereotypes and what is a gay man and what's a lesbian. They came up with the 1970's stereotypes basically, these eight-year-olds in 2014, and I said, "Well, would it surprise you then, to know that I'm gay?" and then literally, I had thirty eight-year-olds gasp in a very dramatic way!

I said, "Well I am, and I'm engaged", and they said, "Noooo, are you gay?" and I went, "Yes", and one of them said, "Is Mr Lee your boyfriend?" and I went, "Yeah! Well done!"

And he was like, "Brilliant; alright cool". And I said, "I was actually really worried about telling you because yesterday a lot of you said that being gay is wrong, but that's *me*." And they were like, "Oh, no, no, no, not *you*!" I was like, "Oh. But, that's what you said." "Oh, but we didn't mean *you*." And I was like, "Well this is what we're talking about. You saying that means *me*", so we unpacked the fact that it's not just a word.

And that was maybe two minutes of the lesson and then it moved straight on to, "When are you getting married? Where are you getting married? Can we sing? Can we come?" And for about a week, it was me going, "It's not appropriate for you to come to my wedding!" They didn't care about the gay thing, they just wanted to know about the wedding, that was it. And my class was boy-heavy, so seventeen boys, thirteen girls, and quite a lot of travellers in our area so we were kind of half expecting a little bit of pushback from the parents, and one parent phoned the school and spoke to the head teacher and said, "Do you think it's appropriate that Mr Ross told the kids that he has a boyfriend?"

And the head just went, "yes".

The next day a little girl brought in a letter. Her mum brought it in and said, "This is from my daughter but she is too, like, scared to give it to you herself", and I was like, "Oh God!" Because this girl is very precocious, she has a lot of her own opinions and it could have been *anything*. So I opened the letter.

ACTOR B Dear Mr R,

Even though you're gay, I will always treat you the same way as I do now. I still think about you the same way as I used to. You're a great teacher and these are just some of the words that I would describe you as: great, amazing, fantastic, brilliant, awesome and brave.

The reason why I say brave is because you shared a personal secret which was very brave.

You don't have to feel scared because I know that everyone in the class feels the same way as I do.

P.S. We are all proud of you.

ACTOR C I had to hand the class over to my TA for a moment while I went outside and shed a quiet, proud tear, and then we just carried on as normal.

And it just became part of the school culture that instead of "gay" being used as a bad word, it's fine. And it's nice. The week after that there was a couple of incidents of people still using it in the playground but the kids started policing themselves really strongly.

The first time it happened this *poor* kid got *frogmarched* to me, you know, like twenty kids around him, like, "Tell Mr Ross what you said."

"I, er, said that something was gay..."

"Oh well, come on then, what is it?"

"There's a boy. On *Eastenders*, I said he was gay."

I was like, "He *is* gay!"

"That's what I said!"

So there were these, like, twenty kids and I had to explain, "*Sometimes* you can call someone gay. Sometimes it's true!"

Everyone thinks you can't talk about it in primary school because they're too young. Actually, it's the perfect time to do it. Children have an innate ease with new information if it's presented as a normal part of society. The idea that I would be talking to these eight-year-olds about sex is ridiculous. I'm just talking about my life.

A Football Fan's Story

ACTOR A (LEICESTERSHIRE) It's my life. Football really is a big part of my life. Yeah, if football was taken away from me I couldn't see what I could do. Always, always, always go down to watch Leicester, I've got a season ticket. I've had a season ticket for years. I suppose it's to do with my family as well 'cause my stepdad, my dad, they're all big football fans, my mum, my granddad, my nanna, they were all big football fans – because my family are all strong football supporters it got put in to me, but I didn't really start playing myself until about sixteen or seventeen, I was a teenager when I started playing whereas my younger brother, he played from a little kid. My little sister, she wants to play football, she's only twelve, my nieces and nephews, they all like football so I think it's to do with the fact that it's a family thing.

At the minute when I go to watch Leicester City play, people at the match don't know I'm gay 'cause we don't really have conversations about sex. It's football, it's football-based, where I sit, we are all season ticket holders, we see each other week in, week out, we don't really ask, "Oh, are you straight? Are you gay?" You know, it's not like that. But the club want to try and start a LGBT fan group for Leicester City, because you have got these fan groups in Manchester, Chelsea, Charlton, so Leicester is trying.

You can't really say there aren't any gay footballers. They're just not out. In a way you can understand because of the abuse, it's still really big in football, homophobia. If racism's still around and that's been years and years since they've been trying to stop it, homophobia... I can't really see that stopping. It's going to take one special person to come out for it to change people's views, if you know if someone like Cristiano Ronaldo come out and said he's gay, if he come out and said he was gay, would he lose his fans? He's the world's greatest football player. But then you think lower down, for example a Leicester City player, who's not known worldwide, if they come out they'd get kicked out of the game, that's more through peer pressure.

When I was playing for my straight football team and I come out to them, I got pushed out of the squad. I'd get to the changing rooms, go and get changed, and then it would be, "Oh, bums to the walls, boys, gay boy's coming through." I used to play constantly first-team football, but I'd see myself put on the sub, used in the last five minutes, or not playing at all. At one point I got chucked out the car on the way back from an away game and I had to ring my dad to come and pick me up. That was it. When that happened I just...I just...I couldn't tell you, there was no phone call or text message or messages to say, "Look, we were just pissing around, I'm sorry." Chucked me out the car and drove off. But that's what I don't like talking about because it's sad really. It shouldn't really happen. It hurt me, I thought they were my friends but obviously they wasn't. But then I got over it, I guess. Found this lot! The Wildcats, an LGB team. Wish I never did, boys!

We play against other gay teams nationally, so we travel the country, we've gone up to Scotland, Wales, and we're all gay and also there's a Midlands league that we play in that are all gay football teams. We do sometimes play straight teams in friendlies and they don't have a problem. We were playing a straight team, can't remember who, and one of our players had gone in for a tackle and missed the ball, so it was a foul but their player stood up, turned around and said, "Oh you fucking faggot." It's part of what it is, if you don't like it, then don't play for the team. His manager did give him a clout round the ear'ole, which was fair enough.

I see it as banter. Even between ourselves, when we're playing games and something happens to one of *our* players and one of *our* players is running funny or does something it'll be, "Oh, you fairy!" You know, where do you draw the line at banter or homophobia, you know? If we can say it to ourselves, so, gays saying it to gays, why should straights not be able to say it in a banter way as well and get away with

it? Where do you draw that line? Is it banter? Or abuse?
It's hard really, ain't it?

A Story About A Funeral

ACTOR C So I get home from work and I go up to my room and you know, you pull your laptop up and I'm playing around on the Internet and I feel something is odd about my computer. So I look on the history and all these photos come up that I'd taken a couple of years before.

Exactly.

So these photos are of me with this guy who I'd met, in slightly awkward positions and wearing slightly awkward outfits. A couple of them are in a leather harness, which I've always been obsessed with. And in a couple I'm sat up and this guys head is between my legs. Yeah.

So I don't really know what to do, so I delete them and go downstairs. Mum is being overly friendly. She's like, "Oh you look tired, go and have your dinner and then when you're finished I need to talk to you about something."

And I say, "No I'd rather just talk about it now because I know what it's about."

"Well," she says. "You know, everyone goes through phases in life darling..."

And blah blah blah and basically, she gives me the get-out-of-jail-free card.

But I think no, I've hidden this too long.

"Mum," I say, "my phase is ongoing and I don't think it's going to come to an end."

So she's like, "If this is a phase and it's over then that's fine, but if you're telling me that this is ongoing then you can't do this. I don't want you here. Get out."

So I do. But it's Friday after work and I don't know what to do or where to go. So I just take some stuff and get in my car and stay out all weekend. Then on Sunday, Mum phones me and she's like, "You've got work tomorrow, you can't be living out your car, come back, don't talk to me and it'll be fine."

I go home that night but when I get there it's horrible because the house is all you know, like, those incense sticks? It's all like that and there's, like, chanting going on in the living room and Mum's wearing all black.

What's going on?

And my mother says to me, "I'm having a funeral for my son."

There's all this Pakistani chanting and stuff. Super religious. Then she says, "I've lost my son and I don't know who you are and that's why you don't need to talk to me, you just need to come back and get on with your life as normal but my son has gone."

And I'm like OK and the thing is, my mum's not even Pakistani, she's Egyptian, and that's not even how we do stuff. We wear white at funerals, but I guess she just wants to be more hardcore than that.

Then. It's four o'clock in the morning I'm asleep in my room and Mum comes into my room and wakes me up, and she's like,

"I want you to go to A and E."

"Why? What happened?" – I think there's some kind of emergency, but my mum's like, "You need to go and get an HIV test, you've got HIV."

"OK Mum, can this wait until the morning and then I'll go?"

But she goes on… "You've got to go, you've got HIV because you're working as an escort."

And I was like, "What?"

I'm a junior doctor! How would I have time to be working as an escort? If I was, I'd be living it up.

But she was just screaming. The whole time they'd told me not to tell my dad 'cause they thought it would break his heart, and there's my mum standing on the stairs screaming, "I can't believe my son sleeps with men, he's disgusting, he's filthy, you're possessed by the devil."

I'm glad I'm not lying anymore, but if I could go back and change it, the way it happened I probably would.

An NGO's Story

ACTOR D How did they find me? I've been involved with the Lesbian Society for about ten years. They got firebombed. They get firebombed quite regularly.

They looked round to see which white people could help them.

There are about 30,000 NGOs in Nepal. We're quite a small NGO, but out of 30,000, I was the only white dyke in town.

Coming out – well it's not a moment; it's not a single moment. Each time you have to make a decision. I'm in a taxi, for example – in...Nepal

ACTOR C (TAXI DRIVER) You're on your own?

ACTOR D Yep.

ACTOR C No husband?

ACTOR D Nope.

ACTOR C Boyfriend?

ACTOR D Nope.

Now... If I say, "Actually, I'm a lesbian."

The taxi driver will say,

ACTOR C A lesbian? Do you have a camera? Record yourself? Can I watch?

ACTOR D So I tend...to say, "I'm a nun."

ACTOR C –

ACTOR D It shuts down the conversation. I can't be fucking arsed to be honest with you.

At a national level I'm quite out. But in the village – if I'm visiting a poor village woman, I don't tell her I'm a lesbian. I don't think she'd fucking know what it was. It would completely blow her mind. I'm there as the director of my NGO.

The primary problem in Nepal for lesbians is that they're women, not that they're lesbian. They're invisible. They're not men. The lesbian thing is seen as another disability, like having epilepsy. It's at that sort of level. It's a problem but it's not the problem. Because if they had confidence, and were able to earn their own money, it's less of a problem.

The whole thing is around the democratization of the country. For hundreds of years the lesbians couldn't speak out, and now they've got their voice and they're demanding. But they don't yet understand how to ask for things in a way that gets a good response.

They get involved with a cow festival, which is a Kathmandu festival, where people come out and do a street dance. So they all get dressed up and put on dildos, go out in the street, rub their dildos in peoples faces and then they wonder why people won't accept them.

Well – you're wearing a dildo, rubbing it in people's faces – this is not a subtle approach. But when you're ready to talk about strategic planning, I'm here for you.

Like all of Nepal – they're good at protesting, they've learnt the art of protest, but they haven't yet learnt the other part of democracy, which is responsibility.

They're very good at "We want this and we want that and we want it now." I helped them write their part of the women's constitution. There is this feeling of "We are special" and I'm like, "Fucking hell."

When we managed to legalize gay marriage for six months, I very quickly married all the Buddhist lesbians together in a room, because I'm a Buddhist priest, so I can do that. You always have a religious marriage, and then it is registered with the government. There's a list then – a list with the government, and that's a risk, especially now that same-sex marriage has been taken back out of the constitution. We talked about that. I said, "Do you really want to do this? Because we don't know what's coming in the future." But they really wanted to do it.

For hundreds of years these women haven't had a voice, they weren't out, but now they have got a voice, they've come out. They are finding their voice, and they're demanding.

A Story About A Yoghurt Spoon

ACTOR A *Midsummer Murders* is on the telly. I'm watching it with Mum and Dad. I'm eating a yoghurt. I think it was a Müller Corner. By the time I've finished this yoghurt I'll have told my parents.

I've finished the yoghurt and I still haven't told them. I start bending my spoon back and forward. Everything's getting a bit overwhelming. The spoon snaps.

My mum looks up from *Midsummer Murders*.

ACTOR D (MUM) You got something you want to tell us, love?

ACTOR A Mum, Dad, I'm gay.

I still have that yoghurt spoon.

An Immigrant's Story

ACTOR B We work with LGBT people who have to flee their country because it's not safe for them to live there. People can claim asylum if there is a threat of serious harm because of their sexuality.

It's been a journey how the law has changed... Up to a couple of years ago the Home Office would tell people, "We believe you're lesbian or gay, but you can go home and be discreet. Go home and don't come out." But then the Supreme Court overturned that. You can't tell them to stay in the closet.

There are new guidelines. You are no longer allowed to ask sexually explicit questions. Just because you have sex with someone doesn't prove your sexuality. Lots of sex workers might have sex with men, it doesn't prove their sexuality.

We work with people to write a personal statement. A statement of somebody's whole life. That's how we judge someone's sexuality – on their whole life, not just on one or two acts. We ask them about their first memories; we ask them when they first realized they were different. We talk about this "difference" a lot. This realization. How did they act on this realization? Did they tell anybody? What was the fear? We build up a whole life story.

The statements are very detailed, so the Home Office can't turn round and say, "This is made up." And they're not about the acts of what happened, more about the feelings of what happened.

What about you? Why did you become involved?

ACTOR D Because it was something I was passionate about. My family tried to "correct" me, so I know.

Having gone through the whole game myself at a time when it was not as easy as it is... Well, you can't say it is easy.

ACTOR B It's different.

ACTOR D It's different.

But back then it was extremely difficult. I did it before 2009. There wasn't a lot of understanding of LGBTI issues at the Home Office.

I did come out before I arrived here but you can't exactly "be out" in a country like Zimbabwe. I was out because of the situation. I was "outed", and it was a case of family trying to get me corrected. Being taken to a faith healer is not a good experience because they try all sorts. The demon casting experience is not pleasant, and it's humiliating as well because there are hundreds of people there. Everyone is shouting, everyone is praying. Trying to cast this demon out of you. It is so intrusive and humiliating. Being forced to drink holy water, being submerged into holy water. It's abusive really.

I didn't want to be corrected. By then I knew it wasn't wrong. There was a time when this lesbian woman was on TV. It had such an impact on me. I was like, "Oh my god nothing is wrong with me", because she was advocating for gay rights, and she was the only gay person there. She had such courage. She went up to the podium and she said, "There are gay black people. I am one of these people." From that day, hearing someone who was out. I didn't think it was wrong. I didn't believe that. I was quite an activist in the making. I was passionate about everything.

ACTOR B A lot of our clients often say they wouldn't chose to come here if they had a choice.

ACTOR D When *I* claimed asylum, you would turn up to the unit and there is a long queue and there are people saying, "What are you here for? And what do you want." So by the time you get to the front you know about everyone and they know about you. And once you're in, there is no privacy. It was like a bank, with people behind glass screens, and the person taking your claim can't hear you and they shout, "What do you want? Why are you claiming asylum?" You'd have to shout. I was OK to tell them, because I was already out. But still, to have to shout something like that, when you are around people from different communities... I'm not a British citizen yet. My current status expires next year, and then I'll apply for indefinite leave to remain.

ACTOR B People walk away with nothing. You give up everything.

ACTOR D And to say you are a refugee, to come out as a refugee. It's a dirty word.

ACTOR B We have support groups that meet up regularly, we tell people to come along and people say, "I thought I was the only gay woman in Uganda", or, "I thought I was the only gay man going through this." And then people learn from being out, from being open with each other. When you're being persecuted, a lot of people think, "I brought this on myself. It is *my* fault I'm being persecuted", and then over time they realize it's not.

An Airman's Story

ACTOR C I've got three medals, one because I came under direct fire from the enemy. Scud missiles landing around all over the place. There was a nuclear, biological and chemical threat. I was out there for six months, serving in the Royal Air Force. Medical Corps.

I met a Norwegian Red Cross worker by the pool at the Diplomat Hotel. We had a brief relationship but I panicked and was like, "Oh God, I've got to break up with him." Then he sat outside my room crying. I just panicked and freaked out. I was scared and broke it off and struggled to explain to the sergeant I was billeted with why this man was crying in the corridor outside our room.

I was leading a double life in the armed forces; I had to, as it remained illegal in the forces to be gay. Just after the war I had a copy of *Gay Times* in my room. It was just in a drawer. They found it and of course they investigated me. For about two years. They bugged my telephone. They called my friends in under caution and all that sort of thing. They bugged my phone. They followed me around. They waited outside the pub. They called me in for questioning. I kept them going for two years.

The MoD's frustration grew and so began some *really* dirty tricks. A last-minute posting for example, to the big spy base in Yorkshire. Suddenly someone had to go away on urgent family business and they needed a medic! They didn't give me any way to get there. And if I *didn't* get there in time, I'd be AWOL. Absent without leave. But I made it. I'm very resourceful.

After a couple of years, I'd had enough. I came out to the MoD in a Court Martial in October 1993. I would finally achieve my fifteen minutes of fame!

Well those were the rules. OK, the rules were crap but those were the rules. I knew it would be six months in detention but I just wanted to get on with it.

The first month in solitary was very much like *The Great Escape*, with my tennis ball in the exercise yard. I've always been a bit of a loner anyway. It's one of the things on my personnel file.

After solitary I got transferred to a small room. Three guys. They found out what I was in there for of course. They were alright. Well, some guys in the room did make threats. But then later on, someone was giving blow jobs for cigarettes and they all rushed out there. Double standards you see.

Before it came out in the press I had to tell my family. My brother has been very supportive, and my mum OK. Then my dad. He always waits to see how everyone else will react. I'm married now. I got married on Tower Bridge. Should have seen the look on my dad's face! But he's come a long way from it being illegal.

So I'm left with a criminal record. In a military prison everyone in there has committed a crime according to the military code of conduct, which is different to the civil code. And when you leave they get to decide whether to actually list it, and what to list it as, because there's no direct correlation between military law and civil law. They're just slightly out. So they get to sit there and say, "Well what is this the closest offence to?" So I'm charged with gross indecency. Same as 1895. The same as Oscar Wilde!

Do I regret my military service? No. It's part of who I am. It made me a stronger person. I have a strong sense of adventure. If I can, I always take a different route when I walk the dog. I've got a cockapoo. He's gay.

The Story About A Note

ACTOR B I came out to my parents after six years of soul-searching. I'd been dreading it for all that time.

I finally set an ultimatum to do it when I was home for Passover. I didn't trust myself to be able to say the words, so I wrote it on a piece of paper.

I walked down the stairs, I walked into the kitchen,

(holds up a note, "MUM, DAD, I'M GAY")

My Mum looked at the note and said, "Well I can't wait to have a daughter in law."

A Drama Queen's Story

ACTOR A I realized I wasn't straight back when I was eleven, perving on a hot maths teacher. Yep they do exist.

But, I didn't tell anyone how I felt as it seemed daft to when you're way below the age of consent, and too risky when you're already being bullied for being the fat/geeky/metalhead/non sporty/gamer/four-eyed awkward mess of the school.

Five years later, and teenage lust kicks in, with a touch of bisexuality. Again, I don't come out as I don't want to scream, "I just want to hump everything."

As I'm still as fat, geeky and awkward as before, I keep my head down, and try to figure out who and what I'm into.

After trying to have a girlfriend, whose sexual advances end up scaring the bejeezus out of me, I soon realize I'm gay, and not a good-looking one at that.

Sixteen-year-old me is confronted with the stereotypes. The guys on dating sites and in porn have six packs, the Scissor Sisters unleash Jake Shears's perfect body on the world, and in comparison, I have more cleavage than *Baywatch*.

So, I start dieting, which soon escalates into a massive battle with anorexia. I go from chunky to skeletal twiglet in less than two months. I'm pale, tired and utterly miserable, so naturally I became an emo.

It's during the emo stage that I start coming out to people. That crowd allows anything, as long as you wear black and listen to enough Marilyn Manson. I soon come out to all my mates. Newfound confidence made it hard to hide, though it was more the obsession with Hello Kitty that gave it away.

Then I hit a wall. I couldn't do the important coming out, to my parents. Sure, I could tell my mates halfway through a game of Mario Kart or at a drunken house party, but using the line, "By the way, I like cock" wouldn't have the same effect on my mum as it did my friends.

More self-induced emo misery occurred. I feel pressured to tell my parents as I feel guilty for lying, but I can't string the words together. I stop eating, sleeping or generally functioning. I look like an emaciated panda, all bones and colossal bags under the eyes. Add teenage hormonal mood swings and I'm an utter joy to be around. I start getting nightmares too, that I'm going to be kicked out, disowned or worse.

Months go by, and I get the courage to say something, until I reach the bottom of the stairs. I bolt up to my PC, blare out some orchestral heavy metal with "deep meaningful lyrics" (I cringe now at why I listened to it), and bawl my eyes out for about two hours.

Once my eyes and throat have dried up completely, I slink down to the kitchen to get a drink then escape. Suddenly, The Mother corners me, snarling.

ACTOR D (MUM) I've had it, what the fuck is wrong with you, child?

ACTOR A I'm gay!

I'm terrified of what's going to come next.

ACTOR D And?

ACTOR A I am mortified.

What do you bloody mean, "and?"

ACTOR D Honestly, Rich. Is that it? You look like a heroin addict, I thought you'd started on smack or something.

ACTOR A I'm still shocked, now assuming this is some cruel trick.

Aren't you going to hit me over the head with a chair and throw me out?

ACTOR D No. Would you like me to? Would it help?

ACTOR A Shock turns to sheer disgust. I've been riding on adrenaline and stress for weeks to come out, and my mum couldn't give two shits. Instead of being relieved, I have a diva fit.

You've ruined my coming out! This is a big moment for me, I've been stressing over this for months. Do you realize how much this means? You utter cow, you can't even let me come out properly! This is supposed to be my moment.

Silence. We stare at each other.

ACTOR D Shall we try this again then?

ACTOR A Please.

I pause, and prepare for theatrics. I howl hysterically.

I'm gay, I'm sorry, I'm gay!

She flings the door open and shrieks—

ACTOR D Get out, you're an utter disgrace. No son of mine is going to be a poof.

ACTOR A I storm out, "Fuck you, you menopausal whore!"

My dad flies out the living room, wanting to see what the hell is happening.

ACTOR D And don't come back! You're no son of mine.

ACTOR A I don't intend to, bitch!

I sashay off.

Few seconds later, I turn around, my mum says—

ACTOR D That better?

ACTOR A Much, thank you.

A Christian Story

ACTOR B I'm an evangelical Christian, and my church is intensely homophobic. Homosexuality is only ever spoken about in lists of sin and shame, compared openly with paedophilia and bestiality, and gay people, the preacher says are—

ACTOR C Idolaters, worshippers of Baal, destined for hell.

ACTOR B I'm sixteen, desperately trying to reconcile my faith with my sexuality, I read and re-read Bible passages and books by people who say being gay is wrong, people who say it's OK as long as you don't actually have gay sex, and people who claim to be "ex-gay". I feel as if the church is telling me I can't be part of it.

So I end up deciding to treat any attractions I had as wrong.

Then one day, I wasn't doing much, just reading a book and suddenly I felt this peace wash over me, and this sense of love and affirmation. It was overwhelming, and I kind of burst into tears, and I sense God saying, "I love you, and you're gay, and I love you. You are my daughter and I made you perfectly." And that changes everything. For the first time, I love who I am, and I become more confident, more happy, more relaxed, closer to God.

I have a strong relationship with the God I have been brought up with, and by. I refuse to let anything come in the way of that relationship, not least the church.

So, I make it my mission to be out in church. So many Christians are prejudiced purely because they have never met a gay person, especially a gay Christian. When I come out to them, most start questioning things they took for granted before – they look at the Bible with new eyes and understanding.

I tell my mother. She had previously been strongly anti-gay, but as I speak this time she listens. She starts to embrace my identity and becomes a fiercely pro-gay advocate within the church. I find myself coming out almost daily to new people, in the church where I work, at parties, in random conversations. It just comes up all the time. Every time, I find my heart beats quicker and my pulse races, in anticipation and fear of rejection or ridicule. But I would gladly take all of that, and the abuse that still sometimes comes my way, to be free, and open, and honest.

THE ACT

CHARACTERS

The Act is written as a one-man play – all of these characters should be played by the same person.

MATTHEW – A somewhat cynical, contemporary, gay man in his thirties.

KENNETH ROBINSON – MP for St Pancras North in 1967, clever and persuasive.

WAITRESS – crafty waitress from Matthews's local greasy spoon

NARRATOR – A noir-ish voiceover of Matthews's life. Narrates at various points

MATTHEWS – A small cog in the Civil Service. In his mid-thirties, he is making little impact on the world. Middle class. Desperate for love.

DEARDRIE – Big-hearted young woman who works on the switchboard in Matthews's office.

EDNA MAY GLADYS ANNE – An older man and habitué of the Soho underground gay scene. He has seen it all, has a wicked tongue and a heart of gold. He is steeped in Polari. Outrageously camp.

NOTES

All characters played by one actor.

House of Commons debates are verbatim.

There was a trend in the 1960s for gay counterculture to rewrite classic songs with dirty lyrics. The original production incorporated these songs, and future directors are encouraged to do so too, with the authors' permission.

PROLOGUE – 2013

MATTHEW I'm having a fight with Adam. I've tried to duck
out of an event he's forcing me to go to. I don't want to go.
I don't like crowds and I don't like people and this will
involve crowds of people. Crowds of gays no less. I can't
stand them. Unless they're handsome. We will fight because
I can't be all charming like he would like me to be and I have
to try and work out whether I should just go and take my
medicine or refuse to and deal with the shit storm from
him. Obviously I'm going to go.

Text alert ping.

That's him. *(He reads aloud.)* Stop being a silly queen and
hurry up. Tom Daley will be there, Dan is hosting and
Ottolenghi's doing the food. And it's only Swedish vodka
so you can get pissed with a clear conscience. Meet me
outside the venue.

Steven's not coming anymore. Steven is in one of those
Twelve Step Fellowships. Not one of the proper ones for
alcohol or drugs or whatever. He's in one because he thinks
he's addicted to relationships with damaged men. It's called
cuntaholics anonymous or something.

Neither of us have any real issues with Steven going to
these meetings – well, it stops him phoning us about his
relationships – it's just he is continually going on about how
the Twelve Steps changed his life. Recently he's found a book
called *The Artists Way*. It's basically the Twelve Steps for
damaged artists, you write letters to your inner artist and
go and look around thrift shops.

Anyway, there was an AA meeting after one of Steven's
meetings and he ran into one of the alchys...a guy called

Ted, I think. They bonded over the beauty of the Twelve Steps. Unfortunately Ted went back out drinking again so Steven's got his hands full trying to fix him or something, so he's no longer free to come to the fundraiser.

Instead we're on a table with Adam, Dan and The Supergays, "Seb and Ian". "Seb and Ian" are friends of ours. And I really hate them. You know the sort. Supergays. Seb works in events and Ian is in PR and they spend a lot of time arguing about what kind of trainers to buy. Friday nights they're out clubbing. Saturdays they have brunch before going to visit the child they're both mentoring, before catching whatever's on at the Royal Opera House. "High–low darling, it's all about the high–low." Apparently that means something. Sundays they sleep it all off and start again on Monday in events and PR. The circle of life! Thank you, Elton.

And they'll want money off us too. It's a Gay Rights fundraiser. I thought we had all the rights?

I certainly don't have any funds, so the whole thing is off to a bad start if you ask me. Even rappers and sports – er – people like us now. Though if Tom Daley was a footballer, I might be more impressed. Diving's about the gayest sport you could ever have. "Mum, Dad, watch me dive into the pool."

Still, Dan hosting, that'll be nice. We haven't seen him in ages, like six months or something. Dan is an actor when he's not hosting things, and recently he's been working in New York. Big successful play in London, gone to Broadway, big success there and now all the cast have got agents there now, and managers. I'll be honest, I don't know what the difference between an agent and a manager is but all of them seem to have both.

Well, Dan was stressing because over in the States his manager told him that it would be a good idea not to come out. So he has been trying to keep his lifelong obsession with men on the downlow. Unfortunately at the same time, back in dear old Blighty, the *Sunday People* was publishing an exposé about him and a Brazilian rent boy called Lukas.

Well, that's it, thinks Dan, America won't have me now, but no! Just you wait a cotton-picking minute. Gay is the new black apparently, literally. The phone hasn't stopped ringing. Jon Stewart. Ellen. Dan returns triumphant to pick up easy gigs like tonight. I might give Lukas a call myself, see if he can't give my career a boost.

The action jumps back in time – we are in the House of Commons in 1965.

HOUSE OF COMMONS

MR KENNETH ROBINSON, *St Pancras North.*

I beg to move, "That this house calls upon her Majesty's Government to take early action upon the recommendations contained in part two of the report of the Wolfenden Committee (Command paper 247 of 1956–57)."

I fully appreciate that this subject is one which is distasteful and even repulsive to many people, including no doubt some honorable members. It is a subject that touches deep and perhaps primitive instincts and which rouses strong emotions, but it is also a topic of some importance not only to the minority who are directly affected by the law but also to the rest of the community. It is for that reason that I chose this subject for debate today.

First of all, I should like to clear up in the briefest possible way some of the misconceptions that are common about homosexuality. I am sorry to take time on this, but in light of things that were said on the last occasion when this subject was debated it is necessary to try to clear the air. It is widely held, for example, that all homosexuals are effeminate, depraved and exhibitionist. This may be true of a very small minority, those of a homopsychopathic character, but after all, much the same could be said *mutatis mutandis* of a small minority of heterosexual people. The majority of homosexuals are useful citizens who go about quite unrecognized and unsuspected by most of us.

They are not confined to any particular social class or professional group. As far as one can discover, they are spread fairly evenly through the population as a whole. There is no evidence whatever, despite widespread belief to the contrary, that homosexuality in this country has increased recently or is increasing. There may be some figures which on a superficial glance might suggest that but research studies reveal no evidence that it is the case.

Homosexuality is seldom a matter of choice for the individual. I understand that it is largely an involuntary deviation, not hereditary but often due to some emotional factor during childhood. I gather that at birth we all of us possess both homosexual and heterosexual elements in our psychosexual make up, but environmental conditions and family relationships succeed in attracting most of us in the direction of normality. Nor, according to most medical opinion, an opinion which is shared by the Wolfenden Committee, is homosexuality a disease. Therefore it is not something which is suitable for medical treatment in the accepted sense of the word. To be fair, however, I should say that there are certain psychiatrists who take the view that there are some types of homosexuality which are a form of neurosis and can be treated by psychotherapy. But I think that it is true to say that the generally accepted view among doctors and sociologists is that this is a disability, a deviation from the norm of the same sort as left-handedness or colour blindness.

I have no wish to suggest that I regard homosexuality as a desirable way of life. It is in my view undesirable, for reasons which I will tell the House. It is undesirable because it leads so often to unhappiness, to loneliness and frustration, because it entails in many cases heavy burdens of guilt and shame on those affected by it and because it seldom provides a basis for a stable emotional relationship. It may also possibly be undesirable on moral grounds because it is a sin, but these are matters on which I am not competent to pass judgement.

Surely all this suggests that these unfortunate people deserve our compassion rather than our contempt, yet we choose to brand them indiscriminately as criminals and to isolate them from the rest of the community...

WAITRESS Seen you last night, coming back at all hours.

NARRATOR Matthews looks down at his egg and chips.

WAITRESS Another late night at the Ministry?

They keep you working all hours, they do. It's not right, not decent.

NARRATOR Matthews tucks into his egg and chips, wanting the waitress to go away, wanting to stop talking. He hates it – the guilt, the shame. He looks intently at this morning's paper, hoping the waitress will leave him alone.

MATTHEWS When did I fall in love?

I fell in love when I was thirteen.

With whom? With Peter. With the usual cliché I'm afraid. A school friend. Blonde. Blue-eyed. Beautiful. He arrived two weeks after everyone else. He'd been on tour with the rugby team from his previous school so already a certain anticipation hung in the air anyway – along with preserving fluid and copper sulphate. So there was an empty space at my particular table in the chemistry room, waiting for him. And a space in my adolescent heart that even I didn't know was there.

I won't bore you with the blue eyes. And the flawless skin, the sweet nature and the golden curls that hung upon his forehead. Or the fact that he played the violin and sang brilliantly. He had all the usual attributes that would launch a thousand ships. And it didn't happen immediately either. We had settled in to a pattern of upbeat jocularity on my chemistry table before one night I had a long and profoundly affecting dream about him. And when I awoke the next day I was afflicted with a burning desire to see him, to make him smile, to give myself over only to his happiness. In short, I was madly in love with him.

I don't want to give you the impression that I was some kind of emotional and sexual somnambulist, that hitherto I had been half alive. Not so at all.

By the age of thirteen I was quite the tart. There had been another boy – not Peter – a boy called Chapman. I wasn't in love with Chapman but I had successfully seduced him through a mixture of charm and cunning. I still blush to think of it. Quite why, I'm not sure.

It took months, I know that. You see, a thousand confidences have to be established before a hand can make a tremulous journey from the back of a friend's head, to his nape, his shoulders, small of the back, buttocks. And a thousand masturbatory fantasies must be endured before one can, in a practical manly way, suggest a little help.

He was a vulnerable boy – his father also dead and mother in the process of marrying for a second time. It was during her honeymoon that Chapman came to stay at my family home. Now, there was a price exacted for this accommodation. I was perfectly bold about this. "If you're going to stay at mine, Chapman, then I get to have a suck every night." And I made good on that threat and more. After a couple of nights I persuaded him to bugger me. I was swathed in blankets and pillows, so that only my rear end was visible. That way he could imagine the girl of his dreams as he worked away on top. Doesn't say much for the girl does it? If she looked like my rear end.

I was sufficiently aware never to expect him to touch me. I loved it and I considered myself quite daring and bold that I could do all this – but I had no ambition beyond it. My eyes were fixed firmly on the act.

There's nothing remarkable about these acts I've described and I might have continued thus into physical adulthood without much thought. Once a year, perhaps, I would ask my wife to stick a Christmas Pudding up my arse just for a feeling of nostalgia. But when I was thirteen I fell in love with Peter and my eyes were raised up to a distant and beautiful horizon. The clouds broke and I was anointed with possibility and romantic ambition.

The Devil, people say, is in the detail and if you are in love with someone, you have to get the basics down like birthdays, place of habitation, siblings names, favourite places, foodstuffs, composers and the names of potential rivals.

I could plan my whole day around his timetable. Around every corner I would spring with a kind word or a tasty morsel to brighten his day. Anything that would illicit his pleasure and reflect it back to me. I lived for it. For him. And when I wasn't with him, especially at night, I would imagine him. Not in a physical way – more like a rabbit in the headlights, stunned and floating and longing.

It became unbearable. Somehow I had to free myself of this burden I carried.

I engaged the help of a third party. A strange boy. His parents were liberals. He would be my intermediary and would carry the life-changing news to Peter that I was in love with him. Duly charged, a day was appointed for this great moment. My friend Whitely would tell my other friend Peter that I, Matthews, the greatest lover since Greek fingers first strummed a lute, *was in love with him*. Which duly he did.

The trouble is, I hadn't really thought any further than that. I think he felt...confusion largely. And certainly about as much excitement as if he'd just been told that the ashtray was in love with the teapot.

Now unfortunately there was nowhere to hide and inevitably the moment arrived when we would see one another again for the first time:

"Hi Peter."

"Hi Matthews."

"I believe Whitely spoke to you. About me. The...thing."

"Yes."

"Well, sorry. About that."

"That's OK."

"And er... Well. Thank you for your understanding."

WAITRESS I seen you last night.

NARRATOR Said the waitress accusingly.

WAITRESS Coming back at all hours.

NARRATOR Matthews looks down at his egg and chips.

WAITRESS Another late night at the Ministry. They keep you working all hours, they do. It's not right, not decent.

NARRATOR Matthews tucked into his egg and chips, wanting the waitress to go away, wanting to stop talking. He hated it, that feeling the morning after a long night – the guilt, the shame. He looks intently at this morning's Telegraph, hoping the waitress would leave him alone.

It had been a long night at the Ministry. Things had been getting more and more difficult in the department since Jeffries took over. Jeffries didn't like Matthews and had made no secret of the fact. "I don't trust him – he's clearly not one of us. Probably an invert, if you ask me. Certainly not a straight up sort of chap."

Matthews hated Jeffries, but most of all he hated himself, because Jeffries was right. No matter how hard he tried to get on with people, to be a good chap, to be one of them, he knew deep down he was different. So he worked harder and harder, stayed later and later, in order to gain the trust of a man who was never going to like him, never going to trust him.

That Tuesday night things had been building up. He felt stressed, tired, unwanted and unloved. He picked up his coat, his umbrella, put on his hat. He passed by Deirdrie on reception, applying her lipstick.

MATTHEWS Off out somewhere nice?

DEARDRIE Me and the girls on the switchboard are heading up west – going out dancing.

NARRATOR Matthews wanted to go dancing with all his heart. Matthews wanted to get tight and dance, and kiss, and... But not with Deardrie, not with the girls from the switchboard.

Outside the rain was coming down. The air was fresh and cold and the pavements glistened as people hurried to catch busses home to wives, to families and nannies, and to cooked dinners.

Matthews put his umbrella up and headed along Whitehall, another anonymous civil servant. Never up for promotion, never destined for great things, not someone to rise through the ranks – a small cog. Not even a cog...cogs are necessary – when a cog fails, the system breaks. The system would do just fine without Matthews.

As he got to Parliament Square he turned right instead of straight on. He turned right, up towards St James, towards Victoria. Not straight on, through Milbank to Page Street, to the Regency Café for dinner, but right towards Victoria.

He didn't know why he'd done that. Just fancied a walk in the rain. Then Victoria turned into St James, then Green Park, then Piccadilly.

He felt his heart start beating, he felt his head start to pound. He was walking quicker and quicker, avoiding the girls in shop windows and the boys leaning up against doors. Where was he going? He didn't know, didn't want to know. He'd turn round soon, he thought, get to the Regency soon so he didn't miss dinner. The lights were piercing him, the sounds, the smells, the filth.

He'd been down these streets a hundred times before. This was nothing new – every time the same, every time inexplicable – the pull – the urge – not thought through, not wanted, an addict unable to control himself. He was terrified of being spotted, terrified of bumping into someone. Finally he darted into a door, down some stairs. Never been there before – but the same, the same as all the others. He burst in and the world seemed to stop.

EDNA Oh Hello! Nice to meet you.

MR KENNETH ROBINSON What is it that the Woolfenden Committee recommends? It is simply that homosexual acts committed in private by consenting adults shall no longer constitute a criminal offence.

Why does the Wolfenden Committee think that the law needs to be changed? I think that there are a number of things amiss with the present law. Perhaps the most important of all is the question of interference with the private acts of adults. I take the view that interference with this sort of conduct by the law can only be justified on very exceptional grounds of public interest. I do not consider that such grounds exists in this case.

Then there are the unparalleled opportunities for blackmail which are inherent in the law as it stands. This is so obvious that I do not think I need labour the point, except perhaps remind the House that the late Lord Jowitt said, based on his experience when he was Attorney General, that in 90 per cent of the blackmail cases that came before him, there were some homosexual components.

Then there are the dubious police methods, which I do not want to go into in detail, to which this law gives rise in certain cases at least. It imposes a very unpleasant burden on the police force and, in my opinion a quite unnecessary burden. There is also the question of unenforceability. I think that it is generally accepted that, to be respected, a law should be readily enforceable, but by their private nature the acts with which this law is concerned cannot – not one in a thousand of them – come to the notice of authority. The prosecutions which take place result from informers, from partners to homosexual acts who turn Queen's evidence, and from confessions extracted by the police.

EDNA Hello.

Nice to meet you.

Oh, how do I do? I do very well, thanks for asking.

I'm judging from the fact that you are shaking like a leaf and you look like you shat yourself that you've never been in here before.

I'm basing that on my in-depth knowledge of psychology and human body language.

And the fact that I come here everyday and I ain't never seen you before.

What's your name?

–

Ooh.

–

Nice name. My mother would like that name. Gentle but strong.

–

My name?

–

Well, as a Royal Duchess you should really call me Your Grace, or Votra Grass, but my real friends use my real name. Edna May Gladys Anne. Edna May for short.

–

How do you do Edna May? I do very well thank you, thanks for asking.

–

Yes you may.

–

Yes you may.

–

Yes you may. Buy me a drink. A whisky and water please.

–

Emmeline, get me hard liquor. Christabelle, a splash of water.

–

We have a somewhat eccentric staff here. Emmeline does the hard stuff. Christabelle does the mixers and the ice when they've got it. They've worked together as long as ever I've been coming and in all that time they've never spoken a word to each other. I think there's a history...

–

Now you're a dolly old thing, aint ya!

–

Dolly old thing, trollin' in here with an eek what launched a thousand ships. Eh? No?
I said: Where'd she come from? I said: Where'd she come from? Lilly Law chasin' her, mark my words. And it's true. They caught her down by the docks sucking on a fisherman's friend and chased her all the way west to Piccadilly.

–

Never mind who I said it to, a friend.

–

She's gone elsewhere, took one look at you and fucked off.

–

She absented herself.

–

Woah woah woah, now before you get all excited about letting me down gently, you ought to know that I'm not even slightly interested in you or your big blue eyes.

–

Like, in this case dear, does not attract like. And you and me are far too similar for that caper. Far too Omi Palone, you are, girl.

–

Far too queer not to put too fine a point on it. Oh come on, don't be precious, precious, I'm not going to spend all night bumping fannies with you, luv, when there's a whole world of real men out there.

–

I'm not that thrilled by cartso if I'm honest. I once went down to that cottage in Leicester Square, Lillybet and Sampson said, "Come on, Edna, it's always rich pickings." So I went and had a varder at what was on offer and the first omi that crossed our path looked, well, pretty nice if you like that kind of thing. So I think, fuck it, Edna, "you're not in Kansas any more", you may as well have a look at his front room. Well. Fully furnished, it was. Fully furnished and curtains and drapes to match. I must confess, virgin that I am, I didn't really know what to do, it was just – there. Sort of nodding at me. Eyeing me up. Honestly, I didn't know whether to smack it one or put it over my shoulder and burp it. Not my cup of tea, dear.

–

You see, I'm really just waiting for my prince. Appreciate I'm in a somewhat difficult situation, given that my ideal man would be a policeman probably, or a fireman or summink, and the single most important characteristic that he could possess is that he would be absolutely not interested in someone like me. He'd want children you see. And, well. I'm barren. Hahahahaha.

NARRATION – MATTHEWS IN THE TOILET

NARRATOR As Matthews leaves the bar, the night air hits
Matthews – he's not ready to go home. He finds himself
walking towards Leicester Square, down the steps and
into the toilet. The smell of stale urine hits him as he
makes his way to a cubicle.

The place is empty.

Silent.

Just the drip, drip, drip of the leaky tap.

He sits and waits.

And waits.

He's beginning to feel a bit silly, a little foolish waiting.
A bit silly. A bit alone.

The mood is dead now...any stirring he once had has
now gone. He's just a man sitting on a toilet waiting for
someone to turn up. Someone he's never met. Someone
who may never show.

Just as Matthews is about to leave, he hears the door
of the toilets swing open. Matthews holds his breath.
He hears footsteps across the tiled floor, sees a pair of
feet walk across the room. They stop, just for a second
by his cubicle.

Boots, not clean, not polished, a little scuffed but not
muddy. Matthews tries to guess the age on the wearer?

He can't guess the age. But the boots – scuffed boots. Can he trust these boots? Or are these boots a trap?

The boots make their way into the cubicle next to his. And wait.

Silence.

Just the drip, drip, drip of the leaky tap.

And then a note.

A note passed under the partition.

Can he trust these boots?

He takes out his pen—

A Parker 45: cheaper than the Parker 21 and sporting a gold nib, as opposed to the old octanium nibs of former Parker Pens.

He writes down the address of his lodgings. His handwriting is messy, shaky, the adrenaline is causing his usually immaculate handwriting to look crude and ungainly.

He passes the note back under the partition, and hurriedly leaves.

But as he leaves, he turns back – he sees a man. Well, a boy – no more than twenty. Scraggy hair and scruffy clothes.

As he walks home, back to his lodgings, he occasionally glances behind him – the boy is there, a little way off.

Following.

MR KENNETH ROBINSON I now turn to the arguments commonly advanced against reform. The first is that if we relax the law in any way relating to private acts, homosexuality will "spread like prairie fire", to use the somewhat emotive phrase of the Honorable Member for Cheadle. Homosexuals will feel free to proselytize and young persons in particular will be endangered to a greater extent than at present. Neither of these assertions is provable or disprovable. All that one can say is that nothing of the kind has happened in those countries which have relaxed their law in the direction in which I am pressing this evening.

I know that some Honorable Members say that the experience of other countries is not relevant. I always wonder why they say that and why they assume that there is something peculiarly depraved in the British character which suggests that we should act differently from say Sweden, which relaxed this law in 1942 and has noticed no difference at all since then.

MATTHEWS Well, erm, thank you. That was...nice.

–

Do you go there a lot? Right.

–

I've never been. Much. Well not recently. It's not the sort of place I would go.

–

Well, obviously if I needed a piss I would. Ha ha. But not where I would go to find a friend.

–

Yes, lots of friends. Good friends. Old friends. Make life worth living, friends.

–

Yes we HAVE only just met, but I would like to think of us as friends. Aren't we? I mean we just did – that.

–

Yes, well, no. I don't do that with any of my other friends. Well, not for a long time. No, no, of course not.

–

Oh, you're teasing me. Oh I see.

–

I just don't do this very much. This. You're not a friend, are you – I mean, I don't know who you are really and I don't know if we have any mutual interests.

–

Over and above.

–

Well, quite.

–

But I'm hoping we can maybe stay in touch, now that we're not quite friends but share one mutual interest. Maybe we could go to the opera or something. Have you ever been to the opera?

–

Well that, the one your mum likes, it's a film about an opera singer. It's not actually an opera.

–

If anything, it's even better. I have tickets for one called *Orfeo*. The hero, Orfeo, goes to rescue his wife. From Hell. She's been murdered, you see, and death has stolen her from him. I find it very romantic. He risks his very soul, and hers, just to hold her in his arms again. Just one more time.

–

No guns, just a lute.

–

Good, we'll go together.

–

Partners in crime.

–

What?

–

Partners in crime... Well, not actual crime...well, yes, actual crime. It strikes me that it's not a crime until/unless/until you get caught. Not like murder or something. If you kill someone then the corpse is still there whether you get caught or not. Our kind of crime doesn't hurt anyone.

–

Very funny!

–

It doesn't. It's just a thing. It builds up over a long time and then its like madness. Can't think about anything else so you meet someone in a *pissoir* and invite them back to your digs. Actually that was a leap of faith – could have just stayed in the *pissoir*.

–

Can I kiss you?

MR KENNETH ROBINSON   It is often said – and one or two newspapers have taken this line – that to change the law would be to appear, at any rate, to condone and encourage homosexuality. Do we condone and encourage adultery, or lesbianism, simply because we have failed to make either a criminal offence?

But the main argument adduced against reform is that public opinion is opposed to it, or is not ready for it. What does this mean? Does it mean that we can never make a change in the law until an overwhelming majority of the people demand that change? If that criterion had been adopted in the past we should still be hanging men for stealing sheep, and still chaining lunatics on beds of straw. A Government are entitled to take into account public opinion; they are entitled to take care that they do not act in such a way as to affront the great majority of the nation. But it is frequently the duty of Government to lead and not to follow public opinion, and to do what they know to be right.

In difficult questions like this, what sort of opinion should they consult before acting? I suggest that it should be the opinion of a reasonable cross-section of the community which has taken the trouble to study the matter intelligently and objectively – and there is no doubt where such opinion lies in this matter. First, I take the members of the Wolfenden Committee. Out of thirteen men and women, described by Sir John Wolfenden as reasonably intelligent people, who began with open minds and spent a fair amount of time assessing the best available evidence, twelve reached the firm conclusion that the law should be changed. I believe that there was no fluke about this. I believe that out of any dozen people who sat down and studied the matter in the same way as the Wolfenden Committee did, on the average ten or eleven would come to the same conclusion.

Then there is the opinion of the Churches, which is to some of us perhaps the most surprising feature of the debate. The Archbishops of Canterbury and York, the Church Assembly, the Methodist Conference and the Committee set up by the Roman Catholic Church to study the same problems as those studied by the Wolfenden Committee all support the same recommendation.

EDNA Hang on the bell, Nelly, what's this? You don't hang about, do you? What have you dragged in now?

Is that a pearl necklace my dear? Pearl necklace and a tiara to match, if I know you.

Not being funny dear but where have you been? I mean, you troll in like a debutante, shakin' like a leaf but as soon as there's a sniff of *(coughs)* cock you're off like a bloodhound. Or a little pig in truffle season. Hahaha well don't be ashamed dear. (**EDNA** *does horrendous pig noises.*) Don't be ashamed of being a little truffle piggy, dear. Coz after all, only the pig gets the truffles!

Piggy! That's your name. Yes it is, you earned it and who's your trade?

Sorry dear, what's your name? I can't get no sense out of her, she's got womb fury. James. My mother would like that name, gentle but strong.

Girls! Come here and meet Piggy and James.

Piggy and James, this is Lilibet, Samson and Michael.

She's called Lilibet after our own dear Queen. Because she's posh and innocent. Or so she says. I've heard it's 'cause her father's got a stammer and her mum's a fat Scottish queen. Either way, she's Lilibet.

Samson – as you can see, she's a big girl. Handy in a scrap, you'd think. And she is, but she's called Samson owing to a medical condition what prevented him from being drafted – fallen arches! But he does his civic duty, he's a guard at the magistrates. Tough as old boots and soft as grease.

And then there's Michael.

Yes, he does have a nickname but it aint polite.

Rubbercunt.

Michael.

He used to be in the Welsh Guards but now he works at my hotel as what they call a porter. He carries things about, that means. It means he can go anywhere in the hotel at anytime and nobody asks any questions. Which is just as well, 'cause he goes to all different rooms at all different times of night, doing favours for our more upper-class guests. Knows most of 'em from his day in the Guards. He's gone from Services to Servicing, if you get my meaning. Apparently he's the best in the business. Rubbercunt Michael.

Now over there is One Bollock Sheila. She has, like Adolph Hitler, only got one ball. Got it shot off during the war. Thinkin' she wanted a fresh start, she sailed to Australia, where she bought a van and a kerosene stove and travelled all over the Outback providing an 'ot dinner to lonely sheep shearers. And anything else they might require in their solitude. Believe me, if all you've seen is red mud and

sheep for six months, you aint gonna be squeamish about
an English queen with one bollock. Quite the business it
was too. "Nosh", she called it. That was all fine until she
got caught by the law and deported. FROM AUSTRALIA!
That puts her in an exclusive club of two. Magwitch and
One Bollock Sheila.

Now, as you'll remember, Michael works at MY hotel. The
Cavendish in Duke Street. Which makes me the Duchess of
Duke Street, so mind your Ps and Qs. Yes, love, on the front
desk, they took one look at me said, "She's exactly what our
customers want to see." No dear, down in the depths is where
I am. Down in the seething, pumping heart of the whole
operation. On the phones, I run the telephone exchange – so
you need never pay for an international call again. Sheila'd
be bankrupt by now if it weren't for me helpin' her keep in
touch with her shepherds and cowboys. I run the phones.

Hello, The Cavendish? To whom shall I connect you?

Good evening, Major. A hot toddy, you say? I'll send Michael
up with it toot sweet.

Within or without the hotel I can talk to anyone at any
time. Keeper of secrets, keeper of reputations. Of course
discretion is the key. I'm never seen and rarely heard and
I never, ever, gossip.

LETTERS

MATTHEWS *retrieves a series of letters and reads them out.*

Dear Jim,

Hope you enjoyed meeting Duchess Edna! I'm still laughing just thinking about it. I'll write with details of the opera shortly. Our night out was wildly enjoyable. Hope the accommodation suited you. It suited me!

Yours,

Dear Jim,

Are not impromptu meetings always the best? Surprised is not the word! After such a grey day at the office, to see you standing outside this evening was like a dream. Though what I will say to Jeffries tomorrow, I can't imagine. Don't worry about the quid I lent you. I think we are beyond that! Everyone forgets things occasionally. I hope it got you home safe and sound.

I'll write with details of the opera shortly.

Yours ever,

Dear Jim,

I am quite given over to the fact that I would do anything for you. Does it seem weak for one man to say that to another? I do not care, I am yours and would do anything for you.

So, you are coming next week on Wednesday at 6:00. I shall be ready for you then. Please make your way up to my rooms, the door will be unlocked. I will be most pleased if you surprise me at my desk. Our tickets are for 7:45, so we will have plenty of time.

There is a finger buffet at Edna's that night (isn't there always), so we'll get to see the girls too.

I'm so desperate to see you. I feel "All Shook Up".

Yours lovingly,

Dear Jim,

Thank you for your company at the opera last night. I hope you found what you saw to be enjoyable. I'm sorry for not making it clear how long it was. And I'm hopeful that your landlady didn't lock you out. The bits you missed I will enjoy telling you about next time. And next time tell her you'll be out all night, did you not do that last time?

Yours,

Dear Jim,

Thank you for your letter. You must be in great torment to have such accusations thrown at you. If I can, as a civil servant, provide a character statement I will certainly do so.

Out of interest, who is the other fellow facing charges? I would be most interested to know. I can only assume he somehow led you into a compromising situation. A respectable person would not do this to a young and impressionable fellow like yourself. You may wish to mention this to your attorney.

Yours,

Dear Jim,

I am desolate without you. Whatever may have happened that night please know that the love I had for you remains, regardless. I miss you so much. Please write back. I long to see you.

Lovingly yours,

Dear James,

My blood ran cold when I read your letter. I must see you
to talk. Whatever you have been offered to implicate me
cannot be worth it. They only want me because of my job,
we'll both be ruined. You're the sprat and I'm the mackerel.
I must see you. I must. And I still miss you.

Yours,

MATTHEWS James. I've missed you.

–

Before we talk I was just wondering if I could ask you to
do something for me. I hope you don't think I'm insane.

–

I just wondered if you would just pretend for a bit that this
wasn't happening and just lie down here with me for a bit?
I thought that if we could just lie down here together for
a bit then we could pretend that everything was fine. Just
for a few minutes we could pretend...

–

You're an arsehole. A fucking arsehole and you're breaking
my heart. And even though you are a tart who leaves me at
the opera to go and...I appear to be in love with you and I
can't just turn it off. To my shame.

–

When I was your age I just assumed that I could never meet
someone. That was just a road that wasn't open to me and
so I threw myself into work and other things. I'm a great
friend to countless people, men and women. Thought that
if I gave enough then I would be happy. All the things that
make life worth living I have taken up with enthusiasm.
And I'm so fucking unhappy. I just have always wanted a
friend. I despair because it seems to me that you can have
all the sex you want, practically in public, only in public

and that's fine. And you can devote yourself to anyone you choose but not go to bed with them.

–

It builds up. My desire to reach out. Until I can't help myself. And then I'll go to any lengths just to touch another body that breathes and is warm and feels warm. And this fantasy I've always had it's, well, it's you. You're beautiful. Your body is warm and sleeps next to me. You are everything I've ever wanted. And you stayed. And you liked me too. And I'm so lonely.

–

I'll do it for you, Jim. I'll take the blame for leading you into it. If you are waiting for me at the other end, I can do it.

–

Or take it back. Tell them you were lying. That you don't know me.

–

And when you get out we can be together. You can get a job near me. We can live together, I can say you're my valet. You can be. The Prince and The Pauper. I could raise you up and you can bring me low and we'll meet in the middle.

–

Jim?

–

It's the best way I can see. By day it'll just look normal. You work for me, you can keep a room for yourself. I'll keep you. And at night, when the rest of the world is asleep, you can creep up and lie next to me. I want that so much, Jim. That way we can lie together every night. Jim?

–

That's not patronizing. I'm not trying to buy you.

–

Oh, because your prospects are so fucking good without me aren't they? Frankly, if I hadn't taken you under my wing, where would you be? Still in that disgusting toilet? You've got nothing. No family. No education. Nothing to fall back on apart from your arse. And I try and raise you out of the slime and you say no thanks. I can't imagine what kind of freedom you are buying with my life. The freedom to piss your life away. It seems my kindness is beneath you. You pass up spending time with me. You leave me sitting on my own in the opera house to go and suck cocks down the dilly. And lie about it. Say it was your landlady...fucking... I knew at the time it was a lie. You're no better than a common prostitute. A thick one too. A dirty-faced whore that sleeps where it shits and then says, "This is nice". I'm sorry, I'm sorry, I didn't mean it.

Can I kiss you?

MR KENNETH ROBINSON I do not believe, as a principle, that the State or the law has any right to interfere with the acts of private individuals, whatever they may be and however much one may dislike them, which have no effect on other people. They are surely a matter of private conscience and not of law, and it is the mark of a truly free country to leave them to conscience and not to the courts.

THE COURTROOM

MATTHEWS Yes.

–

Yes, I confirm that it is my writing.

–

Yes, therefore I wrote it.

–

Well, it is dated 9th July 1965.

–

Well, it is making an arrangement for myself and Mr Moran to see one another.

–

Yes.

–

I'm sorry?

–

Very well.

–

Dear Jim,

I am quite given over to the fact that I would do anything for you. Does it seem weak for one man to say that to another? I do not care, I am yours and would do anything for you.

So, you are coming next week on Wednesday at 6:00. I shall be ready for you then. Please make your way up to my rooms, the door will be unlocked. I will be most pleased if you surprise me at my desk. Our tickets are for 7:45, so we will have plenty of time.

There is a finger buffet at Edna's that night (isn't there always), so we'll get to see the girls too.

I'm so desperate to see you. I feel "All Shook Up".

Yours lovingly,

–

What does it mean? It's a song by Elvis Presley.

–

Sorry.

–

I'm sure that the members of the jury can draw from that letter what they can.

–

I'm not sure I understand what you are insinuating.

–

I was, yes. Very keen indeed to see Mr Moran the following week.

–

Because he was my friend.

–

I enjoyed his company because he was someone whom I believed I could help.

–

I would not use the word inferior.

–

Not deficient in any respect but I enjoyed showing him things he had not seen before. A protégé if you will.

–

Whatever the English for protégé is. Do we not just use the French word?

–

Yes, I am. Highly embarrassed.

–

Because in the normal course of things, one does not expect
to be asked to read back what was written privately.

–

I was very keen to see him. We had become very close in
the weeks preceding that appointment.

–

That is an inference you have made, sir.

–

It would have delighted me to be surprised at my desk.

–

Is that what he says?

–

No. I did not commit any offence against him on that evening
and I fail to see what evidence of it is written in this letter.

–

Obvious to whom?

–

If that is the case, why am I even being questioned?

–

I apologize.

–

Edna is a friend of Mr Moran. I can't remember where.

–

You would have to ask Mr Moran.

–

Whatever you may think of this letter. This letter I wrote.
How is it proof of criminal actions on my part? Am I being
questioned about what I do or what I am?

–

An invert?

–

I'm—

–

An invert?

–

Yes, I am an invert.

–

Yes, I am fully aware that this may colour the jury's view of my character and my life.

–

Their job is to decide whether or not I have committed acts of indecency for which I should be removed from society. But it seems to me that I am not on trial for what I have done but for what I am.

–

I have nothing to lose. And I no longer want the indulgence of a world that would prefer I did not exist. Am I an invert? Yes, I am an invert. And if I never speak another word in my life, at least I will have said this here today. And you must write it down. And report it to your readers. And your families. And perhaps my words will briefly help one frightened child or one lonely man. Rest assured I am not the only invert in this country or in this city or even in the room. We could be anyone. We are your teachers, your doctors, your priests, invisible unless we find the courage to speak out.

EPILOGUE - 2013

MATTHEW Oh God, I feel like shit. I've got a hangover. I've usually got a hangover. But today I've got a post gay rights fundraising hangover and they're the worst!

Adam's asleep. How does he do that? Isn't he anxious?

We had a massive row, obviously. I'm just not gay enough. Or public-spirited enough to care about the new fight for workplace rights or parenting equality or whatever.

Of course by 11:30 the toilets were like Sodom and Gomorrah. That's the trouble with gay men, give them a skinfull and they can't control themselves. You can be as highfalutin as you like during the canapés but by the time the cheese course is over, it all starts to go a bit grotty. And thank God for it. That's the only right I need, thank you very much.

That's the real reason I'm fighting with Adam.

But it's Dan's fault really.

He suggested a little trip to the powder room and then it all goes a bit creamy. But nobody criticizes Dan because he's famous. And handsome. And single. Dan never has to substitute sex for love.

It's certainly not my finest moment. Argh, I just wish it would all go away. Can't we just pretend that everything is normal? If I want to get drunk and have a fumble in the bogs, why shouldn't I? Isn't that gay enough?

The fucking Supergays had everyone enthralled of course. Apparently the boy they're mentoring has given them a whole new perspective on homophobic bullying. Child was upset because someone at school called him gay because he couldn't kick a football well enough. Nine, he is, the poor little shit. So the Supergays told him that he should

ignore bullies who say things like that. That there are gay
people and straight people in the world and that some of
them are sportsmen and some of them are hairdressers
and some of them are lesbians and all of them are lovely
and not to listen to silly bullies who are cowards anyway,
and blah blah blah.

Collective appreciation from the table for the Supergays.
I mean how do you even explain what gay means to a nine-
year-old? I guess you just substitute the word sex with the
word love. Sometimes two people of the same sex just want
to love each other and get married and take out a mortgage
and insurance and buy trainers. And one of them wants to
love the other one up the arse.

It all seems a bit bloodless to me.

FURNITURE AND PROPERTY LIST

A chair (in the original production, this was a white porcelain
    toilet with seat and cover)
A hat stand
A mobile smartphone
A notebook and pencil (for the **Waitress**)
A 1960s radio microphone and stand
A black umbrella
A cigarette holder (for **Edna May**)
Letters in envelopes corresponding to the letters in the script

---

LIGHT EFFECTS AND SOUND

There are not specific sound and lighting cues – it should be
used to help shift the location and mood.

THIS
IS
NOT
THE
END

Lightning Source UK Ltd.
Milton Keynes UK
UKHW02f0621151117
312739UK00006B/210/P